DATE DUE _ 99

ABRAHAM LINCOLN

Roger Bruns

Director of Publications
National Historical Publications and Records Commission
Washington, D.C.

1986
CHELSEA HOUSE PUBLISHERS
NEW YORK
NEW HAVEN   PHILADELPHIA

SENIOR EDITOR: William P. Hansen
ASSOCIATE EDITORS: Jane Crain
John Haney
Marian W. Taylor
EDITORIAL COORDINATOR: Karyn Gullen Browne
EDITORIAL STAFF: Pierre Hauser
Perry Scott King
Howard Ratner
Alma Rodriguez-Sokol
John Selfridge
Bert Yaeger
ART DIRECTOR: Susan Lusk
LAYOUT: Irene Friedman
ART ASSISTANTS: Noreen Lamb
Victoria Tomaselli
COVER: Frank Steiner
PICTURE RESEARCH: Carrie Bruns, Ian Ensign

First Printing

Library of Congress Cataloging in Publication Data

Bruns, Roger. ABRAHAM LINCOLN

(World leaders past & present)
Bibliography: p.
Includes index
    1. Lincoln, Abraham, 1809–1865—Juvenile literature.
2. Presidents—United States—Biography—Juvenile
literature. [1. Lincoln, Abraham, 1809–1865.
2. Presidents] I. Title. II. Series.
E457.905.B78   1986   973.7'092'4 [B] [92] 86-1338
ISBN 0-87754-597-9

Chelsea House Publishers
Harold Steinberg, Chairman and Publisher
Susan Lusk, Vice President
A Division of Chelsea House Educational Communications, Inc.

133 Christopher Street, New York, NY 10014

345 Whitney Avenue, New Haven, CT 06510

5014 West Chester Pike, Edgemont, PA 19028

Photos courtesy of The Bettmann Archive, The Historical Society of
Pennsylvania, Library of Congress, The Smithsonian Institution

Contents

ADENAUER
ALEXANDER THE GREAT
MARK ANTONY
KING ARTHUR
KEMAL ATATÜRK
CLEMENT ATTLEE
BEGIN
BEN GURION
BISMARCK
LEON BLUM
BOLÍVAR
CESARE BORGIA
BRANDT
BREZHNEV
CAESAR
CALVIN
CASTRO
CATHERINE THE GREAT
CHARLEMAGNE
CHIANG KAI-SHEK
CHOU EN-LAI
CHURCHILL
CLEMENCEAU
CLEOPATRA
CORTEZ
CROMWELL
DANTON
DE GAULLE
DE VALERA
DISRAELI
EISENHOWER
ELEANOR OF AQUITAINE
QUEEN ELIZABETH I
FERDINAND AND ISABELLA

FRANCO
FREDERICK THE GREAT
INDIRA GANDHI
GANDHI
GARIBALDI
GENGHIS KHAN
GLADSTONE
HAMMARSKJÖLD
HENRY VIII
HENRY OF NAVARRE
HINDENBURG
HITLER
HO CHI MINH
KING HUSSEIN
IVAN THE TERRIBLE
ANDREW JACKSON
JEFFERSON
JOAN OF ARC
POPE JOHN XXIII
LYNDON JOHNSON
BENITO JUÁREZ
JFK
KENYATTA
KHOMEINI
KHRUSHCHEV
MARTIN LUTHER KING
KISSINGER
LENIN
LINCOLN
LLOYD GEORGE
LOUIS XIV
LUTHER
JUDAS MACCABEUS

MAO
MARY, QUEEN OF SCOTS
GOLDA MEIR
METTERNICH
MUSSOLINI
NAPOLEON
NASSER
NEHRU
NERO
NICHOLAS II
NIXON
NKRUMAH
PERICLES
PERÓN
QADDAFI
ROBESPIERRE
ELEANOR ROOSEVELT
FDR
THEODORE ROOSEVELT
SADAT
SUN YAT-SEN
STALIN
TAMERLAINE
THATCHER
TITO
TROTSKY
TRUDEAU
TRUMAN
QUEEN VICTORIA
WASHINGTON
CHAIM WEIZMANN
WOODROW WILSON
XERXES

Further titles in preparation

ON LEADERSHIP

Arthur M. Schlesinger, jr.

LEADERSHIP, it may be said, is really what makes the world go round. Love no doubt smooths the passage; but love is a private transaction between consenting adults. Leadership is a public transaction with history. The idea of leadership affirms the capacity of individuals to move, inspire and mobilize masses of people so that they act together in pursuit of an end. Sometimes leadership serves good purposes, sometimes bad; but whether the end is benign or evil, great leaders are those men and women who leave their personal stamp on history.

Now, the very concept of leadership implies the proposition that individuals can make a difference. This proposition has never been universally accepted. From classical times to the present day, eminent thinkers have regarded individuals as no more than the agents and pawns of larger forces, whether the gods and goddesses of the ancient world or, in the modern era, race, class, nation, the dialectic, the will of the people, the spirit of the times, history itself. Against such forces, the individual dwindles into insignificance.

So contends the thesis of historical determinism. Tolstoy's great novel *War and Peace* offers a famous statement of the case. Why, Tolstoy asked, did millions of men in the Napoleonic wars, denying their human feelings and their common sense, move back and forth across Europe slaughtering their fellows? "The war," Tolstoy answered, "was bound to happen simply because it was bound to happen." All prior history predetermined it. As for leaders, they, Tolstoy said, "are but the labels that serve to give a name to an end and, like labels, they have the least possible connection with the event." The greater the leader, "the more conspicuous the inevitability and the predestination of every act he commits." The leader, said Tolstoy, is "the slave of history."

Determinism takes many forms. Marxism is the determinism of class, Nazism the determinism of race. But the idea of men and women as the slaves of history runs athwart the deepest human instincts. Rigid determinism abolishes the idea of human freedom—the assumption of free choice that underlies every move we make, every word we speak, every thought we think. It abolishes the idea of human responsibility, since it is manifestly unfair to reward or punish people for actions that are by definition beyond their control. No one can live consistently by any deterministic creed. The Marxist states prove this themselves by their extreme susceptibility to the cult of leadership.

More than that, history refutes the idea that individuals make no difference. In December 1931 a British politician crossing Park Avenue in New York City between 76th and 77th Streets around ten-thirty at night looked in the wrong direction and was knocked down by an automobile—a moment, he later recalled, of a man aghast, a world aglare: "I do not understand why I was not broken like an eggshell or squashed like a gooseberry." Fourteen months later an American politician, sitting in an open car in Miami, Florida, was fired on by an assassin; the man beside him was hit. Those who believe that individuals make no difference to history might well ponder whether the next two decades would have been the same had Mario Contasini's car killed Winston Churchill in 1931 and Giuseppe Zangara's bullet killed Franklin Roosevelt in 1933. Suppose, in addition, that Adolf Hitler had been killed in the street fighting during the Munich *Putsch* of 1923 and that Lenin had died of typhus during the First World War. What would the 20th century be like now?

For better or for worse, individuals do make a difference. "The notion that a people can run itself and its affairs anonymously," wrote the philosopher William James, "is now well known to be the silliest of absurdities. Mankind does nothing save through initiatives on the part of inventors, great or small, and imitation by the rest of us—these are the sole factors in human progress. Individuals of genius show the way, and set the patterns, which common people then adopt and follow."

Leadership, James suggests, means leadership in thought as well as in action. In the long run, leaders in thought may well make the greater difference to the world. But, as Woodrow Wilson once said, "Those only are leaders of men, in the general eye, who lead in action. . . . It is at their hands that new thought gets its translation into the crude language of deeds." Leaders in thought often invent in solitude and obscurity, leaving to later generations the tasks of imitation. Leaders in action—the leaders portrayed in this series—have to be effective in their own time.

And they cannot be effective by themselves. They must act in response to the rhythms of their age. Their genius must be adapted, in a phrase of William James's, "to the receptivities of the moment." Leaders are useless without followers. "There goes the mob," said the French politician hearing a clamor in the streets. "I am their leader. I must follow them." Great leaders turn the inchoate emotions of the mob to purposes of their own. They seize on the opportunities of their time, the hopes, fears, frustrations, crises, potentialities.

They succeed when events have prepared the way for them, when the community is waiting to be aroused, when they can provide the clarifying and organizing ideas. Leadership ignites the circuit between the individual and the mass and thereby alters history.

It may alter history for better or for worse. Leaders have been responsible for the most extravagant follies and most monstrous crimes that have beset suffering humanity. They have also been vital in such gains as humanity has made in individual freedom, religious and racial tolerance, social justice and respect for human rights.

There is no sure way to tell in advance who is going to lead for good and who for evil. But a glance at the gallery of men and women in *World Leaders—Past and Present* suggests some useful tests.

One test is this: do leaders lead by force or by persuasion? By command or by consent? Through most of history leadership was exercised by the divine right of authority. The duty of followers was to defer and to obey. "Theirs not to reason why,/ Theirs but to do and die." On occasion, as with the so-called "enlightened despots" of the 18th century in Europe, absolutist leadership was animated by humane purposes. More often, absolutism nourished the passion for domination, land, gold and conquest and resulted in tyranny.

The great revolution of modern times has been the revolution of equality. The idea that all people should be equal in their legal condition has undermined the old structures of authority, hierarchy and deference. The revolution of equality has had two contrary effects on the nature of leadership. For equality, as Alexis de Tocqueville pointed out in his great study *Democracy in America*, might mean equality in servitude as well as equality in freedom.

"I know of only two methods of establishing equality in the political world," Tocqueville wrote. "Rights must be given to every citizen, or none at all to anyone . . . save one, who is the master of all." There was no middle ground "between the sovereignty of all and the absolute power of one man." In his astonishing prediction of 20th-century totalitarian dictatorship, Tocqueville explained how the revolution of equality could lead to the "*Führerprinzip*" and more terrible absolutism than the world had ever known.

But when rights are given to every citizen and the sovereignty of all is established, the problem of leadership takes a new form, becomes more exacting than ever before. It is easy to issue commands and enforce them by the rope and the stake, the concentration camp and the *gulag*. It is much harder to use argument and achievement to overcome opposition and win consent. The Founding Fathers of the United States understood the difficulty. They believed that history had given them the opportunity to decide, as

Alexander Hamilton wrote in the first Federalist Paper, whether men are indeed capable of basing government on "reflection and choice, or whether they are forever destined to depend . . . on accident and force."

Government by reflection and choice called for a new style of leadership and a new quality of followership. It required leaders to be responsive to popular concerns, and it required followers to be active and informed participants in the process. Democracy does not eliminate emotion from politics; sometimes it fosters demagoguery; but it is confident that, as the greatest of democratic leaders put it, you cannot fool all of the people all of the time. It measures leadership by results and retires those who overreach or falter or fail.

It is true that in the long run despots are measured by results too. But they can postpone the day of judgment, sometimes indefinitely, and in the meantime they can do infinite harm. It is also true that democracy is no guarantee of virtue and intelligence in government, for the voice of the people is not necessarily the voice of God. But democracy, by assuring the rights of opposition, offers built-in resistance to the evils inherent in absolutism. As the theologian Reinhold Niebuhr summed it up, "Man's capacity for justice makes democracy possible, but man's inclination to injustice makes democracy necessary."

A second test for leadership is the end for which power is sought. When leaders have as their goal the supremacy of a master race or the promotion of totalitarian revolution or the acquisition and exploitation of colonies or the protection of greed and privilege or the preservation of personal power, it is likely that their leadership will do little to advance the cause of humanity. When their goal is the abolition of slavery, the liberation of women, the enlargement of opportunity for the poor and powerless, the extension of equal rights to racial minorities, the defense of the freedoms of expression and opposition, it is likely that their leadership will increase the sum of human liberty and welfare.

Leaders have done great harm to the world. They have also conferred great benefits. You will find both sorts in this series. Even "good" leaders must be regarded with a certain wariness. Leaders are not demigods; they put on their trousers one leg after another just like ordinary mortals. No leader is infallible, and every leader needs to be reminded of this at regular intervals. Irreverence irritates leaders but is their salvation. Unquestioning submission corrupts leaders and demeans followers. Making a cult of a leader is always a mistake. Fortunately hero worship generates its own antidote. "Every hero," said Emerson, "becomes a bore at last."

The signal benefit the great leaders confer is to embolden the rest of us to live according to our own best selves, to be active, insistent, and resolute in affirming our own sense of things. For great leaders attest to the reality of human freedom against the supposed inevitabilities of history. And they attest to the wisdom and power that may lie within the most unlikely of us, which is why Abraham Lincoln remains the supreme example of great leadership. A great leader, said Emerson, exhibits new possibilities to all humanity. "We feed on genius. . . . Great men exist that there may be greater men."

Great leaders, in short, justify themselves by emancipating and empowering their followers. So humanity struggles to master its destiny, remembering with Alexis de Tocqueville: "It is true that around every man a fatal circle is traced beyond which he cannot pass; but within the wide verge of that circle he is powerful and free; as it is with man, so with communities."

—*New York*

1

Gettysburg

It was a crisp November day in 1863. The 15,000 people assembled in the broad field were restless. On the edges of the crowd, there were seemingly endless rows of coffins. Further off, skeletons of horses were visible among the stumps of blackened and broken trees.

At last, a tall, bearded man, dressed in black, rose to his feet in front of the crowd. He started to speak, his voice as clear as the crack of a rifle. "Fourscore and seven years ago," he began, "our fathers brought forth on this continent a new nation. . . ." The crowd remained riveted in silence until his final words: ". . . that government of the people, by the people, for the people shall not perish from the earth." Then a roar of applause thundered across the rolling farmland.

The address, which contained 10 sentences, had taken three minutes to deliver. The speaker was Abraham Lincoln, 16th president of the United States. The place was Gettysburg, Pennsylvania, where, some four months before, 7,000 Americans had died under their own countrymen's fire in the nation's great Civil War. The occasion, as Lincoln had just said, was the dedication of "a final resting

This photograph of Abraham Lincoln (1809–1865), 16th president of the United States, was taken shortly before his assassination. His haggard appearance testifies to the immense strain under which he had labored in his tireless endeavors to bring the Civil War (1861–65) to a just and enduring conclusion.

The Confederate flag, which the armies of the rebelling Southern states carried into battle against federal forces during the Civil War. The flag features the "Stars and Bars" design used by the Confederacy from 1861 to mid-1863.

The rotting corpses of soldiers killed in action litter the fields around Gettysburg, Pennsylvania, following the desperate and bloody battle that was fought there in July 1863 between 88,000 Union troops commanded by General George G. Meade (1815–1872) and the 75,000-man Confederate Army of Northern Virginia led by General Robert E. Lee (1807–1870).

place for those who here gave their lives that that nation might live."

Gettysburg, the most celebrated battle of the Civil War, was one of the most savage ever fought on American soil. More than 50,000 men were killed or wounded in this titanic clash between the armies of Confederate General Robert E. Lee and Union General George G. Meade. Lee, eager to achieve final victory for the rebelling Southern states, had decided to invade the North. A participant later recalled "bullets hissing, humming, and whistling everywhere: cannon roaring; all crash on crash and peal on peal, smoke, dust, splinters, blood, wreck, and carnage indescribable." The battle noise, one soldier remembered, was "strange and terrible, a

A tattered Confederate flag is held aloft during the Battle of Gettysburg. The resounding defeat suffered by the Confederate forces at Gettysburg dealt the Southern states' military potential a blow from which it was never fully to recover.

This painting of Lincoln delivering the famous address that he gave at Gettysburg in November 1863 now hangs in the state capitol building in Springfield, Illinois, where Lincoln embarked upon his political career. In his speech, which dedicated a burial ground to those who had perished at the Battle of Gettysburg, Lincoln declared that it was the duty of the living to continue "the unfinished work" of defending freedom.

sound that came from thousands of human throats . . . like a vast, mournful roar."

The bodies of thousands of soldiers remained unburied for months after the awesome battle. The resulting call for a proper cemetery led to the November 19, 1863, ceremony at which Lincoln delivered his stirring promise "that these dead shall not have died in vain."

Lincoln had worked hard on the speech. He had not, as legend has it, jotted it down on the back of an envelope on the train to Gettysburg. Although many in the crowd, including some reporters, were puzzled by the brevity of Lincoln's address at

Gettysburg, the speech would later be inscribed on monuments, printed in countless publications, memorized by generations of schoolchildren.

In 267 words, Lincoln had captured the spirit of a nation that was proud of its heritage and devoted to its system of law. In the midst of the horror wrought by the war, Lincoln appealed to the finest aspirations of his countrymen. At a time when the emotional divisions between the two sides remained seemingly irreconcilable, Lincoln called for a national rebirth based on brotherhood. No trace of sentimentality or partisan rancor tainted the magnificent address that Lincoln gave that day. Lincoln had spoken plainly and directly:

"Fourscore and seven years ago our fathers brought forth on this continent a new nation, conceived in liberty and dedicated to the proposition that all men are created equal.

"Now we are engaged in a great civil war, testing whether that nation, or any nation so conceived and so dedicated, can long endure. We are met on a great battlefield of that war. We have come to dedicate a portion of that field as a final resting place for those who here gave their lives that that nation might live. It is altogether fitting and proper that we should do this.

"But, in a larger sense, we cannot dedicate, we cannot consecrate, we cannot hallow, this ground. The brave men, living and dead, who struggled here, have consecrated it, far above our poor power to add or detract. The world will little note, nor long remember what we say here, but it can never forget what they did here. It is for us the living, rather, to be dedicated here to the unfinished work which they who fought here have thus far so nobly advanced. It is rather for us to be here dedicated to the great task remaining before us—that from these honored dead we take increased devotion to that cause for which they gave the last full measure of devotion—that we here highly resolve that these dead shall not have died in vain—that this nation, under God, shall have a new birth of freedom—and that government of the people, by the people, for the people, shall not perish from the earth."

Lincoln's cadences sang the ancient song that where there is freedom men have fought and sacrificed for it, and that freedom is worth men's dying for. For the first time since he became president he had on a dramatic occasion declaimed, howsoever it might be read, Jefferson's proposition which had been a slogan of the Revolutionary War—"All men are created equal"—leaving no other inference than that he regarded the Negro slave as a man. His outwardly smooth sentences were inside of them gnarled and tough with the enigmas of the American experiment.
—CARL SANDBURG
American poet and biographer of Lincoln, writing about the Gettysburg Address

Four score and seven years ago our fathers brought forth, upon this continent, a new nation, conceived in Liberty, and dedicated to the proposition that all men are created equal.

Now we are engaged in a great civil war, testing whether that nation, or any nation, so conceived, and so dedicated, can long endure. We are met here on a great battle-field of that war. We have come to dedicate a portion of it as a final resting place for those who here gave their lives that that nation might live. It is altogether fitting and proper that we should do this.

But in a larger sense we can not dedicate— we can not consecrate— we can not hallow this ground. The brave men, living and dead, who struggled here, have consecrated it far above our poor power to add or detract. The world will little note, nor long remember, what we say here, but

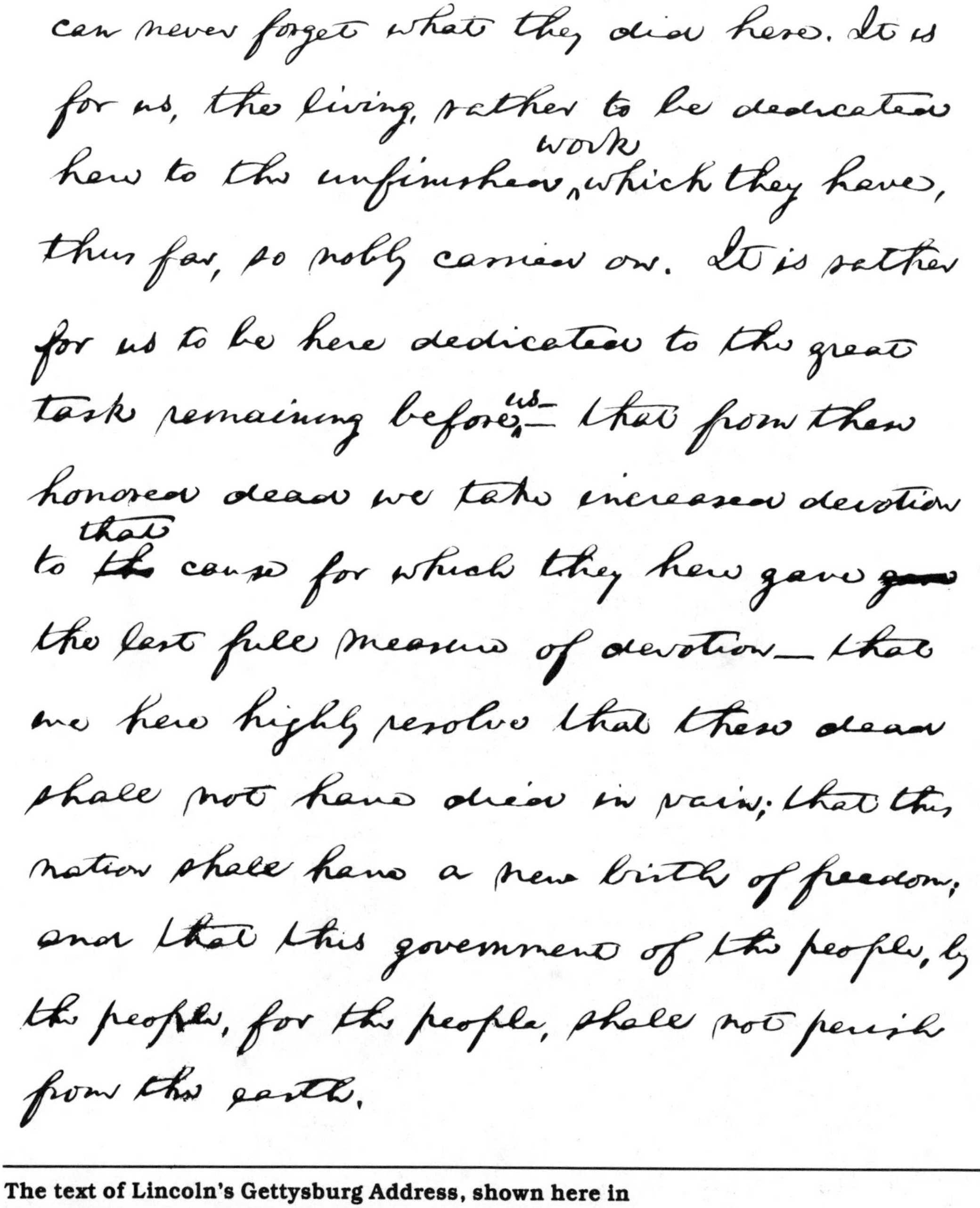

can never forget what they did here. It is
for us, the living, rather to be dedicated
here to the unfinished work, which they have,
thus far, so nobly carried on. It is rather
for us to be here dedicated to the great
task remaining before us— that from these
honored dead we take increased devotion
to the cause for which they here gave
the last full measure of devotion— that
we here highly resolve that these dead
shall not have died in vain; that this
nation shall have a new birth of freedom;
and that this government of the people, by
the people, for the people, shall not perish
from the earth.

The text of Lincoln's Gettysburg Address, shown here in
the president's own handwriting, contains just 267
words. In this speech, which has been memorized by
generations of American schoolchildren and inscribed
on monuments throughout the country, Lincoln clearly
expressed his determination to preserve the Union.

2

Frontier Roots

Approximately a mile southwest of the White House in Washington, D.C., where Abraham Lincoln spent the last years of his life, is a memorial. Its white marble columns rise majestically; an inscription reads: "In this temple, as in the hearts of the people for whom he saved the Union, the memory of Abraham Lincoln is enshrined forever."

Inside the rows of columns of the Lincoln Memorial is an imposing 19-foot statue of a brooding Lincoln looking across Washington toward the United States Capitol. Every year, hundreds of thousands of people visit the memorial, gaze at the splendid statue, wander between the enormous columns, and read again some of the words spoken by the man in whose honor the monument was erected.

Of all America's leaders, Abraham Lincoln has been perhaps the most celebrated. During the 12 decades that have passed since his death, his life story has been told and retold, shaped and reshaped by writers, poets, and playwrights. The images are rich and varied; the myths abundant. Through it all, Lincoln has remained a figure of power, a commanding historical presence, a symbol deeply

Lincoln's stepmother, Sarah ("Sally") Johnston, whom his father married in 1819, when Lincoln was 10 years old. Although Lincoln was extremely devoted to his family during his childhood and youth, he became increasingly eager to leave the frontier life behind and to set out on his own.

The young Lincoln, depicted here with ax in hand, spent much of his youth splitting fence rails and chopping firewood on the frontier in Indiana. According to American novelist Herman Melville (1819–1891), President Lincoln shook hands ". . . like a man sawing wood at so much a cord."

IN THIS TEMPLE
AS IN THE HEARTS OF THE PEOPLE
FOR WHOM HE SAVED THE UNION
THE MEMORY OF ABRAHAM LINCOLN
IS ENSHRINED FOREVER

Carved by American sculptor David Chester French (1850—1931), this imposing statue of Lincoln greets visitors to the Lincoln Memorial in Washington, D.C. Hundreds of thousands of people flock to the monument each year to see the 19-foot marble statue of one of America's greatest presidents.

rooted in the American spirit.

In spite of the stories, the hero worship, and the tributes, Lincoln remains an elusive figure. In his lifetime, he was never fully understood even by his friends. Complex, driven by conflicting moods and tensions, in many ways lonely and private, Lincoln always defied easy characterization.

To some he was a simple, prairie westerner who enjoyed spinning tales from the frontier; to others he was a crafty politician, carefully manipulating the prejudices of the people for his own political gain. Some saw him as an unsophisticated and unlettered backwoods farmer; to others he seemed uncommonly perceptive, and exceptionally well educated. Lincoln's quick wit and homespun sense of humor, sharpened by a strain of deep melancholy, have become legendary. He was a compassionate man of peace who, as president, found it necessary to use force and violence to achieve his ends. Lincoln worshiped the principles of law and yet as president he suspended certain basic rights guaranteed by the Constitution. To those people who wanted to end slavery immediately, Lincoln seemed a foot-dragger, uncommitted to the cause of black people. To those who were passionately devoted to a way of life that depended on the enslavement of blacks, however, he was the devil himself, bent on destroying that way of life.

No leader in the nation's history has had to endure such agonies in governing as those that beset Lincoln. He faced conflicting duties and overwhelming burdens. Of all the stories of American leaders, Abraham Lincoln's is one of the most extraordinary.

Born on February 12, 1809, in Kentucky, where his father and grandfather had moved in the first wave of settlers to cross the Appalachian Mountains, Lincoln lived his early days in a log cabin on the frontier. Much of his boyhood, he once wrote, was spent swinging an ax. One of Lincoln's earliest memories was being told of his grandfather's death at the hands of Indians. Lincoln's father, Thomas, worked at many odd jobs, especially carpentry; like many of his fellow pioneers, he could neither read nor write.

A new kind of historian would be required to comprehend the genius of a character so externally uncouth, so pathetically simple, so unfathomably penetrating, so irresolute and yet so irresistible, so bizarre, grotesque, droll, wise and perfectly beneficent as the great original thinker and statesman Abraham Lincoln.
—quoted from an editorial in the *New York Herald*, 1865

When Lincoln was seven years old, his father moved the family to Indiana. His mother, Nancy, died there two years later. In 1819 Thomas Lincoln married Sarah Johnston, a widow with three children. Lincoln always remembered his stepmother with warm affection.

Black-haired, lean and lanky, the youngster grew up with a reputation for great physical strength. He was also, some thought, a bit lazy. However, Lincoln's apparent laziness was actually a result of the measures to which he had to resort in his efforts to educate himself. While he was plowing his father's fields, Lincoln would carry books, snatching time to read while his lathered horses rested. A cousin, reminiscing about the days he and Lincoln worked the fields, remembered him returning to the house after a day's work, grabbing a piece of cornbread, sitting down, propping his long legs up as high as his head, and burying himself in books such as *The Adventures of Robinson Crusoe* or *Aesop's Fables*, or books on English grammar. He also read the Bible, which he enjoyed not only for its stories and characterizations but for its rich poetic style.

Although Lincoln received only about a year of formal education in Kentucky and Indiana, he managed to become an educated, well-read man. He did it mainly on his own—by borrowing books and composing verse. With each new volume, he became more resentful of the frontier's lack of intellectual activity. When he left the frontier behind, he did so with a vengeance. In later years he often expressed scorn for the mindless, physical drudgery he had known in his youth. For Lincoln, the life of the prairie was a life to be overcome.

For a time, Lincoln worked as a helper on a ferry boat and occasionally brought Ohio River steamboat passengers ashore in his own skiff. In 1828, when he was 19, he rode down the Mississippi River all the way to New Orleans on a flatboat. The eager, wide-eyed youngster was beginning to see much more of the world than the back of a plow.

Determined to push out into the world on his own when he reached age 21, Lincoln helped the family with one more migration. In March 1830 the Lin-

The little advance I now have upon this store of education, I have picked up from time to time under the pressure of necessity.
—ABRAHAM LINCOLN

colns loaded their plows and hoes onto ox-drawn wagons and set off for the black-loam country of Illinois. There, along the Sangamon River some 10 miles west of Decatur, they fenced 10 acres, broke ground, and began to raise corn.

Lincoln now had the remarkable physical characteristics that fascinated almost everyone with whom he came in contact. He was almost six feet, four inches tall. He had coarse, black hair, a dark complexion, and deep-set gray eyes shielded by

An 18- by 16-foot replica of the log cabin Lincoln grew up in marks his birthplace in Hardin County, Kentucky. The young Lincoln disliked the drudgery of life on the frontier and was deeply frustrated by the lack of intellectual activity that the pioneer existence had to offer.

heavy, black eyebrows. His nose was prominent and slightly askew, his cheekbones high, his mouth wide, his ears large. A contemporary reporter for the London *Times* wrote: "It would not be possible for the most indifferent observer to pass him in the street without notice." Although Lincoln was often photographed, none of his pictures, according to people who knew him, captured the magnetic quality he projected in person. Describing Lincoln's face, the poet Walt Whitman wrote: "Of technical beauty it had nothing—but to the eye of a great artist it furnished a rare study, a feast, and fascination."

Lincoln's gangly, uncoordinated appearance was deceiving. His exceptional strength made him a swift runner and superb wrestler. Even when he was 50 years old, he could lift an ax with one hand and hold it in front of him at shoulder level (a feat that sounds much easier than it is).

If Lincoln was an unusual physical specimen, he also exhibited uncommon qualities of mind. He wrote poetry and read Shakespeare, Lord Byron, and the historian Edward Gibbon. He was passionately interested in logic and mathematics. A standard text on geometry by the ancient Greek mathematician Euclid later became favorite reading.

Lincoln was also fascinated by law. He began to spend time in the log courthouses, listening as country lawyers delivered their summations, hearing tobacco-chewing old-timers discuss legal cases and the techniques of influencing juries. To young Lincoln, the atmosphere of the courtroom was intoxicating.

Although skeptical of organized religion, Lincoln believed in a God who controlled human destiny. He was morbidly interested in death, fearful of dreams, and superstitious. In January 1828 his sister Sarah died in childbirth. Although death at an early age was not unusual in those days, losing his sister, with whom he had been very close, was difficult for the young Lincoln to bear.

In 1831 Lincoln began working as a clerk to a storekeeper and mill owner named Denton Offutt, in the small town of New Salem, Illinois. At the age of 22, Abraham Lincoln was on his own.

Not often in the story of mankind does a man arrive on earth who is both steel and velvet, who is as hard as rock and soft as drifting fog.
—CARL SANDBURG

American poet Walt Whitman (1819–1892), author of *Leaves of Grass*, eulogized Lincoln in his poem "O Captain! My Captain!" and described Lincoln's features as an artist's "feast." Those who knew Lincoln felt that photographs failed to capture his personal magnetism.

3

New Salem

In moving to New Salem, Lincoln had not left rural Illinois. He was still on the prairie, still separated from the world of ideas and learning that he craved. But he was away from his family, able now to make his own way in life.

As he worked in Offutt's store, Lincoln traded jokes and stories with the farmers, and made friends with some of the young men who congregated in the town's two saloons. Although he was now part of a fairly rowdy group, Lincoln left liquor alone. It made him, he said, "flabby and undone," and he wanted to avoid anything that threatened his self-control or blurred his mind.

At James Rutledge's tavern he met the proprietor's daughter, Ann, a pretty, auburn-haired 19-year-old. The two became close friends. Lincoln greatly respected Ann's father, who owned a library of some 30 books and ran a local debating society.

A profile of Lincoln emphasizes his prominent nose and his large ears. His distinctive physical characteristics, including his lanky six-foot, four-inch frame, often made a considerable impression on anyone meeting him for the first time.

Lincoln sits and talks with a friend in New Salem, Illinois, where he lived between 1831 and 1837. Although he was defeated in his first political contest, running for the Illinois state legislature in 1832, the amiable candidate had, in the course of his campaign, greatly impressed the voters with his keen intelligence and his uncompromising candor.

When Offutt's business soured, Lincoln, searching for a more exciting area of enterprise in which to exercise his abilities, decided to try politics. An avid reader of newspapers, he was becoming knowledgeable about national affairs as well as local issues. He entered the field of candidates for the state legislature in 1832. Mounting boxes to give outdoor speeches, slapping backs in taverns, pitching horseshoes with the voters on Sunday afternoons, Lincoln campaigned vigorously.

Lincoln offered the voters a plan for opening up the Sangamon River for commercial transport. He also spoke out strongly in favor of public schools,

A 19th-century painting shows steamboats and flatboats on the Mississippi River. At age 19, Lincoln, who had already had some experience of piloting a skiff, traveled aboard a flatboat to New Orleans, Louisiana.

The statehouse in Springfield, Illinois, where Lincoln attended legislative sessions for four consecutive terms following his election to the Illinois state legislature in 1834. During his period as a state legislator, Lincoln gained the respect and admiration of colleagues and constituents alike.

declaring that every man should receive "at least a moderate education and thereby be enabled to read the histories of his own and other countries, by which he may duly appreciate the value of our free institutions."

Lincoln had read much American history. From his early years behind a plow to the days in Offutt's store, he had been inspired by the words and deeds of America's founding fathers. He would later say

that his entire political philosophy could be traced to the Declaration of Independence, which insists that all men, regardless of their background, have the right to freedom and liberty, the right to achieve according to their ability.

In announcing his candidacy for the state legislature, Lincoln said to the voters, "I am young and unknown to you. I was born and have ever remained in the most humble walks of life. I have no wealthy or popular relations to recommend me. My case is thrown exclusively upon the independent voters of this county, and if elected they will have conferred a favor upon me, for which I shall be unremitting in my labors to compensate."

Lincoln did not win that election. But he carried New Salem by a large majority, impressing many voters with his knowledge of public affairs, and making them laugh with his "crackerbarrel" stories.

Although he had failed in his bid for the state legislature, Lincoln was by no means through with politics. But, for now, his own distressed financial condition demanded action. He had enlisted in the militia that summer, volunteering to join an expedition to drive a group of Sac Indians across the Mississippi River. Elected captain of his company, Lincoln led his fellow recruits across the Illinois prairie for several weeks, never once encountering a hostile Indian. They did, on one occasion, find several scalped men—a grisly sight that greatly disturbed Lincoln. But he was able to joke later about these days of military service, saying that in the defense of his state he had, indeed, shed blood—that of mosquitoes.

Having thus established the beginnings of a political reputation, Lincoln was able to get himself appointed part-time postmaster of New Salem. He also earned some income as an assistant to the county surveyor, a job that increased his already keen interest in geometry.

Lincoln later became a partner in a general store with a local businessman named William Berry. Lincoln spent more time talking politics than minding the store, while Berry, a heavy drinker, concentrated on the whiskey barrel in the back room. The

> *If the good people, in their wisdom, shall see fit to keep me in the background, I have been too familiar with disappointments to be very much chagrined.*
> —ABRAHAM LINCOLN
> in a speech that he delivered while campaigning for the Illinois state legislature in 1832

store failed, Berry died, and Lincoln was left with a debt of over $1,000. Gradually, he repaid all of the money, an action that increased his reputation for honesty among the people of the county.

In 1834 Lincoln decided to run for the state legislature again. During this period, there were two parties fighting for national supremacy: the Democrats, led by President Andrew Jackson, and the Whigs, led by Senator Henry Clay of Kentucky. Lincoln admired Clay, and became a Whig. He was attracted to Clay's ideas of forging national unity through strong federal programs, especially in the area of transportation. Lincoln saw the need to provide the country with a network of railroads, turnpikes, and canals. Such a system, he believed, would offer the means for vigorous national expansion.

Lincoln's second try for elective office was a success. Placing second in a field of 13, he joined three other Whigs from Sangamon County in the Illinois House of Representatives. He was 25 years old.

When the legislature adjourned in February 1835, Lincoln rode back across the freezing, windswept prairies to New Salem. He was determined to study diligently for a career that would not only make the best possible use of his knowledge and skills but might also lead to greater political opportunity. He decided to become a lawyer.

Although most law students worked with accomplished attorneys in preparing for the bar, Lincoln taught himself. He memorized Blackstone's *Commentaries* (a standard work of jurisprudence), and rehearsed cases aloud to himself. To the people in and around New Salem, many of whom read little or nothing at all, Lincoln seemed something of a bookworm. They were amused by the sight of the six-foot, four-inch man lying on the ground, his long legs propped on a tree, his nose in a law volume.

In August 1835 Lincoln once again had to overcome personal anguish. Ann Rutledge, his friend from New Salem, died at the age of 22. How quickly, Lincoln brooded, are human happiness and dreams obliterated. Friends remembered his sinking into deep depression, which sometimes plagued him for weeks at a time. But he always found a way out of

> *Upon the subject of education, not presuming to dictate any plan or system respecting it, I can only say that I view it as the most important subject which we, as a people, can be engaged in.*
> —ABRAHAM LINCOLN
> in his first public speech,
> March 9, 1832

it, usually by plunging deeper into work and study.

Lincoln soon stood before the Sangamon County examiners, passed his legal examinations, and became a practicing attorney. His first case, a typical one for the prairie, involved a dispute over ownership of some oxen and farmland.

Lincoln would serve in the state legislature four times, gaining increased recognition with each passing session. His sharp intelligence, keen insight, and droll humor cheered his Whig allies and disarmed his opponents. He was now familiar to most state lawmakers and was fast becoming a force in state politics.

With his increased prominence and political power, each new issue he faced seemed to take on greater importance and to present a greater challenge. During the 1836–37 legislative session, Lincoln came face to face with an issue that would haunt him for the rest of his life. It was one that lay at the center of his own future as well as the future of the country. It was the issue of slavery.

A mounted overseer supervises slaves working on a cotton plantation in the South during the early 19th century. It was during his second term in the Illinois state legislature that Lincoln became increasingly aware of the intensity of the ideological conflict between the Northern abolitionists and the Southern slaveowners, and of the fact that the slavery issue might eventually tear the country apart.

4

The Fire-Bell Rings

Whenever there is a conflict between human rights and property rights, human rights must prevail.
—ABRAHAM LINCOLN

In the Declaration of Independence, Thomas Jefferson, the United States' third president, wrote that "All Men are created equal." Forty-four years later, in 1820, as 11-year old Abraham Lincoln tilled the fields of his family's small Indiana homestead, Jefferson, now 77, was living at Monticello, his plantation in Virginia. The former president was still close to national affairs, still exercising his remarkable insight and learning. As he read of the battles in Congress over the possible extension of slavery in the country, Jefferson became increasingly concerned about the terrible divisions that the issue was creating in American society. He warned of the extreme dangers that lay ahead. The question of slavery, he said, filled him with terror, "like a fire-bell in the night."

For over two centuries blacks had been brought in chains from their African homes to America, where they had been bought and sold, worked and beaten. Despite the vigorous efforts that various political and religious leaders had made to end the practice, the institution of slavery had become firmly entrenched in America. With Eli Whitney's

Slaves toil in the fields on a cotton plantation in the South. Throughout the 19th century much of the cotton grown in America's southern states was purchased by Britain, which boasted a flourishing and immensely profitable textile industry. As Southern planters expanded the scale of their operations to meet the British demand, increasing numbers of slaves were imported from Africa.

A 19th-century engraving shows blacks being sold at a slave auction as free blacks look on in tears. In 1837 Lincoln expressed his disapproval of the system of slavery in a strongly worded protest to the Illinois state legislature, in which he declared: "The institution of slavery is founded on both injustice and bad policy."

> *I hate slavery because it deprives our republican example of its just influence in the world, enables the enemies of free institutions with plausibility to taunt us as hypocrites, causes the real friends of freedom to doubt our sincerity, and especially because it forces so many good men amongst ourselves into an open war with the very fundamental principles of civil liberty, criticizing the Declaration of Independence, and insisting that there is no right principle of action by self-interest.*
> —ABRAHAM LINCOLN

invention of the cotton gin in 1793, cotton manufacturing became even more profitable than it had been, and Southern planters became even more dependent on the labor of black slaves.

Slavery, while widely accepted, did not lack for opponents. Those people who considered slavery morally wrong and wanted to see it abolished had become a major political force. The abolitionists, as these opponents of slavery were known, were concentrated in the North and had incurred the hatred of slaveowners with their demand that all slaves be released immediately. From the year 1800 on, a series of slave uprisings had struck fear into the hearts of Southerners.

Hoping to prevent further slave rebellions, Southern legislators enacted numerous laws to limit the rights of slaves. They expanded their military resources and embarked on a campaign to suppress abolitionist publicity.

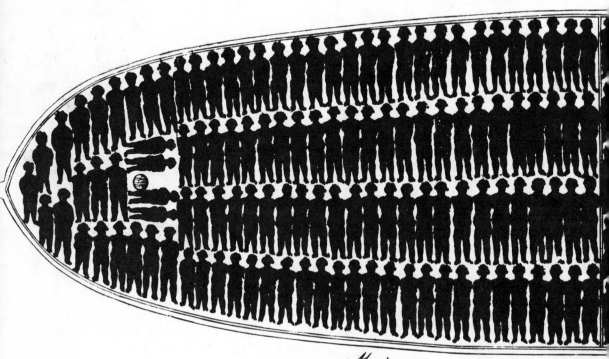

Men's room

By the time Abraham Lincoln entered his second term as a representative in Illinois, several Southern states had sent petitions asking the legislature to suppress abolitionist protest. The petitioners called the abolitionists dangerous lunatics, and claimed that the South had a sacred right to own Negroes. If slaves were set free, the Southerners claimed, blacks would sweep into the Northern states, a prospect that surely the Northerners must fear and wish to prevent.

Most legislators in Illinois sympathized with the Southerners. Illinois whites generally opposed abolition efforts, fearing an influx of blacks into the region and a subsequent mixing of the races. The state had already enacted laws that prevented blacks from voting, holding political office, sitting on juries, or even attending schools. Although the Illinois state constitution outlawed slavery, poor blacks, desperate for food and a place to sleep, often sold

A 1789 drawing of a slave ship shows how each captive was allocated only a few feet of space. At one point in the text of the book in which this picture first appeared, the writer declared that the helpless Africans were packed aboard such vessels "to the state of being buried alive."

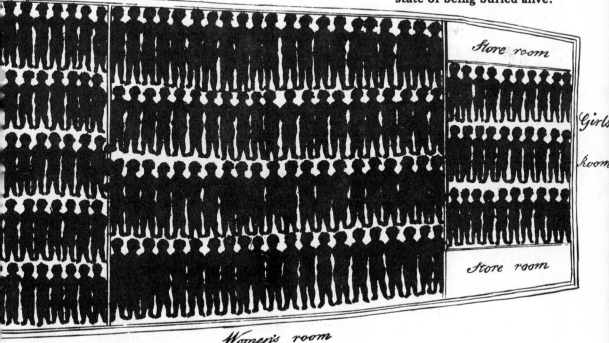

Slaves operate a cotton gin. Until 1793, when this machine was invented by Eli Whitney (1765–1825), cotton seeds were separated from the fiber by hand, a time-consuming and not particularly cost-effective process that yielded approximately one pound of pure cotton per worker per day. Following the invention of the cotton gin, however, rates of production increased by a factor of 50.

themselves as "indentures" for 20 years, a form of voluntary slavery. Illinois was hardly a haven for the abolitionists and their antislavery sentiments.

Responding to the Southern petitions, the Illinois legislature passed a series of resolutions condemning the growth of abolition societies. Seventy representatives voted in favor of the resolution; six voted against. Abraham Lincoln was one of the six.

Lincoln felt so strongly about the issue that he, along with one other legislator, submitted a formal protest to the legislature in March 1837. "The institution of slavery is founded on both injustice and bad policy," the protest charged. All his life, Lincoln believed slavery to be morally wrong. The great problem was how to end it.

To Lincoln, slavery seemed directly opposed to the ideas of liberty and equality, which were enshrined in the Constitution. Like Jefferson, Lincoln saw the conflict over slavery as the one thing that could tear the country apart. Like Jefferson, he believed that slavery would gradually self-destruct because of its immoral nature and eventual impracticality. He also believed that it would be better for the blacks themselves to be sent out of the country, and be "colonized" in Africa or some other location.

Although he opposed slavery, Lincoln did not believe that the government had the right to force the South to give up its slave system. He did not favor the tactics of confrontation employed by the abolitionists, fearing that passion over the issue would lead to increased violence.

Lincoln's worst fears were soon to be realized. In 1837 Elijah Lovejoy, editor of an abolitionist newspaper in Alton, Illinois, was murdered by a mob. The killers also burned his office and threw his printing press into the Mississippi River. John Quincy Adams, former president of the United States, declared that Lovejoy's murder was "a shock as of any earthquake throughout this continent." In such mob violence and hatred, young Lincoln saw the seeds of national conflict that threatened to undo the work of the founding fathers, to overthrow the nation's devotion to law. Thomas Jefferson's vision of a fire-bell in the night was taking on a grim reality. It was a reality that would plague Abraham Lincoln for the rest of his life.

> *I have always thought that all men should be free; but if any should be slaves, it should be first those who desire it for themselves, and secondly those who desire it for others. Whenever I hear anyone arguing for slavery, I feel a strong impulse to see it tried on him personally.*
> —ABRAHAM LINCOLN

Angry slaveowners set fire to a warehouse owned by an abolitionist. Lincoln's fears that the slavery issue would lead to escalating violence were realized in 1837, when Elijah Lovejoy (b. 1802), editor of an abolitionist newspaper, was murdered by proslavery activists in Alton, Illinois.

5
Springfield Attorney

In 1837 Lincoln left New Salem for Springfield, a city of 2,000 people that was soon to become the capital of Illinois. John Todd Stuart, a young Whig politician, invited Lincoln to join him as a law partner, and Lincoln accepted with enthusiasm. He was gradually making his way from a life on the prairie to a rising career in law and politics.

During the next four years, Lincoln and Stuart built a rather substantial law practice. Their office, located over the store where the state circuit court met, was equipped, Lincoln remembered later, with "a small dirty bed, one buffalo robe, a chair and a bench." As his practice grew, so did Lincoln's understanding of the intricacies of the law. The tall young attorney from rural Illinois began to establish a sound reputation.

Lincoln lived above a general store owned by Joshua Speed, a burly Kentuckian who was, like Lincoln, a bachelor. The two men became close friends; they often spent their evenings swapping stories with other men at the back of the store. However, even with his quick wit, his gift for storytelling, and his ability to see humor where others could not, Lincoln was a lonely man, tormented by self-doubt.

Lincoln is portrayed here as a young lawyer and aspiring politician, c. 1835. In 1837 Lincoln left New Salem for Springfield, Illinois, where he soon became much sought-after for his legal talents and also grew more determined to break into politics at the national level.

Lincoln entertains his friends at the back of the general store above which he lived during his early years in Springfield, where his devotion to the principle of law deepened as he further immersed himself in his work as an attorney.

Lincoln and his first law partner, John Todd Stuart (1807–1885), at work in their sparsely furnished office in Springfield. It was during the lifetime of this partnership (which lasted from 1837 until 1841) that Lincoln began to gain a reputation as an expert attorney and a likely candidate for political advancement.

Speed once remarked, "I never saw so gloomy and melancholy a face in my life."

In December 1839 Lincoln attended a formal dance in Springfield. There he met Mary Ann Todd, the witty and flirtatious daughter of an influential Whig banker from Lexington, Kentucky. Although he was usually ill at ease around women, especially if they were as elegant and cultured as Mary, Lincoln was immediately taken with her grace and charm, and her knowledge of literature and politics. She was now living with her sister Elizabeth, and Elizabeth's husband, Ninian Edwards, a wealthy Springfield socialite. Lincoln soon became a frequent caller at the Edwards mansion, much to the dismay of Elizabeth and Ninian, who regarded Lincoln as a crude backwoodsman, an unsuitable match for the pretty and popular Mary.

Mary was 21, eight years younger than Lincoln.

Like him, she was intelligent and sensitive. Just as he had, she had lost her mother at a very early age and often felt lonely and insecure. Her background, however, was worlds apart from his. Pampered, used to wealth and its trappings, Mary was very much a young woman of society; she observed formal etiquette, danced the stylish steps, and was always beautifully dressed. She had studied literature and French at a fashionable academy. She also had a fiery temper, and was known for her outbursts and tantrums.

Although they came from very different back-

Mary Ann Todd (1818–1882), the pampered daughter of a wealthy Kentucky banker, seemed an unlikely match for the plain and unsophisticated Lincoln, whom she first met in 1839. Although Mary's family objected to the young couple's involvement, Lincoln and Mary were eventually married on November 4, 1842.

grounds, Abraham Lincoln and Mary Todd were strongly attracted to one another and soon decided to marry. Highly displeased, the Edwards family made it clear to the awkward suitor that his attentions were unwelcome.

Lincoln, already deeply insecure and embarrassed by his lack of formal education and knowledge of the social graces, was devastated. He sank into one of the greatest emotional crises of his life. At the Edwardses' insistence, he broke off the engagement with Mary. One friend remembered Lincoln looking haggard and drawn for weeks, barely speaking above a whisper. He told his partner, Stuart, "I am now the most miserable man living."

Deeply depressed by the broken engagement, Lincoln once again found comfort in his work. He had formed a new partnership with a fellow state legislator named Stephen Logan, and now he worked frantically on one legal case after another. The firm of Logan and Lincoln was soon one of the most sought after in Springfield.

By the summer of 1842, Lincoln had recovered his self-confidence, and he decided to see Mary Todd again. After their year and a half of separation, the two young people found they were more in love than ever and, despite Mary's family's objections, they set a wedding date. The Edwardses finally gave in, and on November 4, 1842, the 33-year-old lawyer and his 25-year-old sweetheart became Mr. and Mrs. Abraham Lincoln. Engraved on the wedding ring that Lincoln placed on his bride's finger were the words: "Love is Eternal."

The couple spent their first year of marriage in a single room that Lincoln had rented at the Globe Tavern for four dollars a week, including meals. For Mary Todd Lincoln, who had grown up amid luxury, getting used to living in a modest tavern was not easy.

Living at the Globe was but one of several adjustments that Mary had to make in her new role as Mrs. Abraham Lincoln. On August 1, 1843, she gave birth to a son, Robert. The following year, with help from Mary's father, the Lincolns bought a comfortable house in Springfield, a move that consid-

Lincoln's perceptions were slow, cold, clear and exact. Everything came to him in its precise shape and color. No lurking illusion or other error, false in itself, and clad for the moment in robes of splendor, ever passed undetected or unchallenged over the threshold of his mind. He saw all things through a perfect mental lens. There was no diffraction or refraction there.
—WILLIAM HERNDON
junior partner in Lincoln's
Springfield law practice

The Lincolns moved to this house, located on Eighth and Jackson Streets in Springfield, in 1844, a year after their first son, Robert, was born. Lincoln and Mary's devotion to one another was passionate: Lincoln sometimes described Mary as "my child wife," while Mary considered Lincoln "lover—husband—father, *all*."

erably increased the couple's sense of security. Two years later, another son, Edward, was born.

In 1844 Lincoln and Stephen Logan dissolved their partnership. Logan took his son as a junior partner, and Lincoln selected a young attorney named William Herndon as his new junior associate. Herndon, who was nine years younger than his 35-year-old boss, had studied law in the Logan and Lincoln office. Hard-drinking, intelligent, a nonstop talker, and something of a rogue, Herndon was to become Lincoln's closest professional ally.

Neither of the new partners was neat by habit, and their law office was in a perpetual state of chaos; important papers were scattered and stacked on tables, chairs, floor, and even in Lincoln's stovepipe hat. A local joke had it that orange seeds left over from Lincoln's lunches sometimes sprouted in the thick layer of dirt on the office floor.

Lincoln's trial work was in Illinois' eighth circuit, an area of 14 counties in the central part of the state. Twice a year, the state's judges rode the circuit, trying cases in remote county seats. Many Springfield lawyers, including Lincoln, followed the judges on horseback; sleeping in primitive quarters, braving flooded rivers and contending with bouts of malaria, Lincoln and the others spent months on the road every year. Although riding the circuit disrupted his family life, Lincoln gained many new friends and political contacts during his travels.

In 1845 Lincoln decided to run for Congress. He rode through his congressional district that summer, gathering endorsements from Whig party leaders, and at the party's 1846 district convention, he was nominated by acclamation.

Lincoln's Democratic party opponent, a circuit-riding Methodist clergyman named Peter Cartwright, accused him of atheism. Lincoln admitted that he was not a church member, but he asserted that he believed in a supreme being, and had never denied the truth of the Bible. He won the election.

With his wife and two sons, the Illinois lawyer left Springfield for Washington, D.C., in 1847. He was now the Honorable Abraham Lincoln, congressman from Illinois.

A 19th-century photograph of a Springfield street shows the house (to left of drugstore) named for Stephen T. Logan, Lincoln's second law partner, with whom he worked between May 1841 and December 1844.

6
Washington

Bﾞritish novelist Charles Dickens, visiting Washington in 1842, wrote of "avenues that begin in nothing and lead nowhere. . . ." Another British visitor, writer Anthony Trollope, was even less charmed, calling the capital "as melancholy and miserable a town as the mind of man can conceive."

Into that town, early in December of 1847, came a recently elected congressman from Illinois. Except for the fact that his pants barely reached his ankles, Abraham Lincoln looked the part of a legislator. The Illinois wilderness was behind him at last. He was ready to take on the nation's capital. Lincoln's initial impressions of the city were little different than those of Dickens and Trollope. He saw Pennsylvania Avenue, dotted by gullies and pits, where small cyclones of dust ripped into the faces of carriage riders, before turning into mud and slush in the rain. Near the White House, there were slaughterhouses surrounded by foraging pigs and sheep; rotting wooden sheds, privies, and a foul creek were all that interrupted the gaping open spaces. Downtown, Lincoln saw slave pens, where manacled black men, women, and children waited to be sold, "precisely,"

Democrat James K. Polk (1785–1849), who became the 11th president of the United States in 1845, declared war on Mexico in 1846. Lincoln, who thought the war completely pointless, was quick to condemn Polk's policies as those of "a bewildered, confounded, and miserably perplexed man."

Following his election to the U.S. House of Representatives in 1847, Lincoln almost wrecked his career in national politics at its outset. He offended many of his colleagues and constituents by denouncing the Mexican War (1846–48), which he considered immoral, unjust, and part of a Democratic party plot to add new slave states to the Union.

he said later, "like a drove of horses." The sight filled him with revulsion.

The Lincolns found accommodation in a boardinghouse, across the street from the unfinished, wooden-domed Capitol. Lincoln enjoyed spinning his after-dinner tales with other Whig congressmen lodged at the inn, and he immediately threw himself into his work in Congress. Mary, however, found nothing to like in the bustling, untidy city, or its society. After three months, she packed up the boys and went to stay with her father in Lexington.

When Lincoln arrived in Washington in 1847 the United States had just decisively defeated the Mexican army of General Antonio Lopez de Santa Anna and, through a peace treaty with the Mexican government, was about to annex territories totaling 1,193,061 square miles. President James K. Polk, a Democrat, insisted that the war with Mexico had been justified, that Mexican soldiers had attacked Americans and that the United States had acted in self-defense.

A majority of Whig politicians, including Lincoln, had serious doubts about such claims. With the addition of vast new areas to the United States, there arose the paralyzing question of whether or not slavery should be allowed in the new territories.

Lincoln charged Polk and the Democrats with having incited an "immoral and unnecessary" war in order to add new slave states to the Union. The new congressman from Illinois introduced resolutions and gave spirited speeches attacking Polk.

Politically, Lincoln did himself enormous damage. Back home in Illinois, Democratic newspapers marveled at his stupidity, calling him a defender of the "murderer and butcher" Santa Anna, and accusing him of disgracing the state by his "treasonable assault" on the president.

Before he had accepted the Whig nomination to Congress, Lincoln had agreed not to run for a second term, so that other Whig politicians could occupy the post. He had counted, however, on being appointed commissioner of the federal General Land Office at the end of his two-year term. The political fallout that resulted from his vehement de-

If you once forfeit the confidence of your fellow citizens, you can never regain their respect and esteem. It is true that you may fool all the people some of the time; you can even fool some of the people all the time; but you can't fool all the people all the time.
—ABRAHAM LINCOLN

The Alamo, an old Spanish mission in San Antonio, Texas, was the site of a bloody battle for Texan independence from Mexico in March 1836. The 188-man Texan force was wiped out, but Texas was to become an independent republic just six weeks later when Texan forces led by General Sam Houston (1793—1863) crushed the Mexicans at the Battle of San Jacinto on April 21, 1836.

An American cavalry unit commanded by Captain John
May charges a Mexican redoubt at Resaca de la Palma in
1846. The Mexican army, which was poorly trained and
supplied, was no match for the American forces, and
Mexico lost almost half its territories during the course
of the 17-month war.

The U.S. Capitol as it appeared during Lincoln's two-year term (1847—49) in the U.S. House of Representatives. The dome that now caps the building was placed in position in 1862, the second year of Lincoln's first term as president.

nunciation of the Mexican War was so great that, to his bitter disappointment, he was not offered the General Land Office job. Despite this setback, Lincoln hit the campaign trail in support of other Whig candidates, visiting states as far north as Massachusetts. His message was clear: only the Whig party could stop the spread of slavery. After a speech in Boston, the *Daily Advertiser* described him as "very tall and thin . . . with an intellectual face, showing a searching mind and cool judgment." He spoke at rallies across New England, in New York, and on through the Midwest to Chicago. Even without a government position, Lincoln was now well known to voters across the North.

In 1849, two years after his arrival in Washington, Lincoln was back in his Springfield law office. His first experience with national politics had been brief, but his passion for political battle, his skill at debate, and his sense of justice remained undiminished. Washington had not seen the last of Abraham Lincoln.

7

A House Dividing

> *What I do say is that no man is good enough to govern another man, without that other's consent.*
> —ABRAHAM LINCOLN

Lincoln's partner, William Herndon, had kept their law firm while Lincoln was in Washington. The office across from the Springfield courthouse was a welcome sight to the ex-congressman. Lincoln again threw himself into his work, taking on new clients, renewing old acquaintances, repairing the damage to his popularity caused by his blistering attacks against Polk and the Mexican War.

Lincoln was soon arguing cases before the Illinois Supreme Court, the federal courts, and the state circuit courts. He represented such large corporate clients as the Illinois Central Railroad and the McCormick Reaper Company. He also continued to take on such ordinary cases as suits for slander, divorce, or patent infringement. He accepted local clients as they appeared, forging new friendships and earning the respect of increasing numbers of people.

The Lincolns continued to live in the modest house on Eighth Street, its backyard containing a privy, a tethered cow, a weedy garden, and a small stable complete with horse and buggy. Never very interested in clothes, Lincoln always wore a plain black suit, carelessly knotted necktie, and his sig-

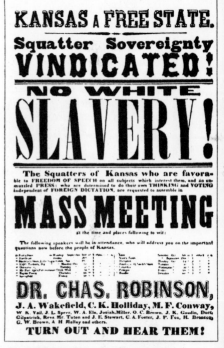

An 1854 poster declares support for the fact that, under the terms of the Kansas-Nebraska Act, which was introduced by Senator Stephen A. Douglas (1813–1861) in 1854, the residents of the Kansas Territory would be allowed to decide for themselves whether or not slavery would be allowed within that territory.

In 1849, at the end of his two-year term in Congress, Lincoln returned to his law practice in Springfield. Of Lincoln's tendency to hide his deepest feelings with regard to matters both public and private, a colleague once said: "He always told only enough of his plans . . . to induce the belief that he had communicated all, yet he reserved enough to have communicated nothing."

nature hat, a black stovepipe that added several inches to his tall, loose-jointed frame. He often took his sons to the office, where, Herndon noted with annoyance, they "rifled drawers and riddled boxes." Lincoln would work at his desk seemingly oblivious to the commotion around him. He adored the boys and was as indulgent a parent as neighbors and friends had ever seen—much too indulgent, it seemed to Herndon and many others.

The bond of affection between Lincoln and his wife remained strong. Each tolerated the other's tendency to anxiety and moodiness. Lincoln still suffered from occasional bouts of depression, and Mary was often tense and highly emotional, losing her self-control over the most trivial incidents. Lincoln's frequent absences from home while riding the circuit were especially distressing to her. But each was a great source of comfort to the other in times of need.

One such time occurred in 1850. After a two-month illness, Eddie, the Lincolns' beloved four-year-old son, died on February 1. Robert, his older brother, later remembered his mother's immense grief and her weeks of constant weeping. He recalled the sadness that descended over the household, and his father's dark and haggard look. The family slowly recovered from the shock of the youngster's death—Mary finding comfort in religion, Lincoln losing himself in his work. He took on new cases, kept himself informed about local and national political issues, and made a few speeches. Less than a year after Eddie's death, a third son, Willie, was born. Three years later, the Lincolns' fourth and last child, Thomas, was born.

Back in Washington, debate on the slavery issue was becoming increasingly heated. At last, the leading Whig statesman, Senator Henry Clay, steered through Congress a series of resolutions designed to preserve the peace between North and South. This legislation, which became known as "the Compromise of 1850," made concessions to both the antislavery and the pro-slavery factions. Clay's legislation also admitted California as a free state (a state without slavery), and allowed the newly formed

With all Lincoln's awkwardness of manner and utter disregard of social conventionalities that seemed to invite familiarity, there was something about Abraham Lincoln that enforced respect.
—JOHN HAY
Lincoln's private secretary

Lincoln, pictured here with his son, Thomas (who was nicknamed "Tad"), was a loving and indulgent father to his four sons. The early deaths of his sons Edward (1845–1850) and William (1850–1862) left Lincoln and Mary deeply saddened. Tad survived his father, but died, at age 18, in 1871.

territorial governments of New Mexico and Utah to make their own decisions about the legality of slavery. It banned the slave trade in the District of Columbia, and provided for a new and more vigorous law requiring that escaped slaves be returned to their masters.

Lincoln silently watched from Illinois. He wondered if the compromise had solved anything. He feared that the pro-slavery Southern "fire-eaters" and their Northern abolitionist enemies would continue to stir the nation's passions, driving the country toward a terrible confrontation. Yet Lincoln still felt that the majority of Southerners wanted slavery no more than he did. He still hoped that the Union could be preserved through reasoned debate and enlightened leadership.

In 1854 Lincoln's optimism proved to have been ill founded. The delicate political balance between the supporters and opponents of slavery was violently upset by the furor that erupted over Senator Stephen A. Douglas's Kansas-Nebraska Act.

"The Little Giant," as Douglas was called (he was just over five feet tall), was a brilliant orator. This dynamic and popular Illinois Democrat had a significant national following and a burning desire to be president of the United States.

Like many politicians confronting the slavery controversy at that time, Douglas had been searching for a solution that would soothe national tensions. He thought he had found it in an idea he called "popular sovereignty." The concept was simple enough. The residents of new territories—in this case, Kansas and Nebraska—should decide for themselves whether to allow slavery.

Although the idea seemed fair and democratic on the surface, Lincoln thought it dangerous. Opening up new areas for possible expansion of slavery, he reasoned, would stimulate violent competition to settle the land. He was also convinced that the North had no intention of allowing slavery in the new territories. The North wanted settlers, he said in a typically colorful turn of phrase, to have "a clean bed, with no snakes in it."

"Bleeding Kansas" soon proved Lincoln's fears

> *I think I have no prejudice against the Southern people. They are just what we would be in their situation.*
> —ABRAHAM LINCOLN
> speaking in 1854

well founded. Kansas Territory became a fierce combat zone of ballots and bullets. Antislavery leaders from New England recruited new settlers to move to Kansas; Southern pro-slavery leaders did the same. What followed was a head-on collision, featuring rigged elections, guerrilla warfare, and murderous lynch mobs. In Kansas, sectional hatred over slavery flared as never before, foreshadowing the bloodbath that was to engulf the nation a few years later.

The situation in Kansas sparked unprecedented violence in the United States Senate. After delivering a vituperative, two-hour anti-Southern speech entitled "The Crime Against Kansas," Senator Charles Sumner of Massachusetts was bludgeoned with a cane by Preston Brooks, a representative from South Carolina, on the Senate floor. Sumner suffered serious injuries.

The Kansas-Nebraska Act fueled Abraham Lincoln's political fires. He began to travel across Illinois, speaking against Douglas's "popular sovereignty" doctrine, insisting that it threatened to undermine the goals of Jefferson and the other founding fathers, who had wished to limit the growth of slavery.

To farmers showing off cows and hogs at state fairs, to crowds gathered in small town squares, Lincoln railed against the Kansas-Nebraska Act. In Peoria, he talked about the evil of a system that gave certain black people no more rights than animals. It was, he said a "monstrous injustice." However, Lincoln still refused to condemn the Southern slave-owners personally. They had not originated the slave system, he said; they were, instead, trapped in it.

In 1855 Lincoln decided to try for a political comeback by running for the U.S. Senate. For weeks, he tramped through Illinois, sleeping little, distributing copies of his Peoria speech, meeting with state political leaders. He was unsuccessful. Illinois was not yet ready to elect to the Senate a Whig with antislavery sentiments. But Lincoln had made a creditable attempt, and was gracious in defeat. His political stock in Illinois was again on the rise.

> *As a nation, we began by declaring that all men are created equal. We now practically read it, all men are created equal except Negroes. When the Know-nothings get control, it will read, all men are created equal except Negroes and foreigners and Catholics. When it comes to this I shall prefer emigrating to some country where they make no pretense of loving liberty— to Russia, for instance, where despotism can be taken pure, and without the base alloy of hypocrisy.*
> —ABRAHAM LINCOLN

During his senatorial race, Lincoln still called himself a member of the Whig party. That party, however, was dying. The Whigs had suffered embarrassing defeats in the early 1850s, and differences of opinion among its members about the Kansas-Nebraska Act led to its becoming hopelessly splintered. As the slavery controversy deepened, the nation's party structure would come more closely to reflect the divisions that had been created by that single, burning issue.

On February 28, 1854, at a meeting in a Ripon, Wisconsin, schoolhouse, the Republican party was born. The new party, which was committed to the principle of keeping slavery out of the new territories, was highly attractive to Lincoln. By 1856, he was campaigning hard for the Republican party's first presidential candidate, John C. Frémont, who was running against Democrat James Buchanan of Pennsylvania. Lincoln spoke to huge crowds, including one of 20,000 people at a state fair in Alton. As he argued passionately to keep slavery out of the new territories, Democratic newspapers in Illinois began to brand him the "high priest of abolitionism." Rejecting the fiery name-calling and threats that had now come increasingly to characterize public debate throughout the country, Lincoln called for a return to the principles of the American Revolution. He urged the American people to seek national harmony and to repudiate violence.

Many Southern leaders were now threatening to take their states out of the Union and to set up a separate government, with the slave system as its cornerstone. Lincoln tried desperately to shake off what he called the "bear hug of disunion." National unity, he believed, lay at the very heart of the country's past and would determine its future. "We won't dissolve the Union," he said to the South, "and you shan't," because "we won't let you."

James Buchanan won the election by a small margin and carried Illinois. The Republicans, however, captured the governorship and four out of nine congressional seats. At a gala banquet in Chicago, the Republican faithful celebrated their surprising showing. Lincoln declared that the central issue in the land was that of equality. The country, he said, must move steadily forward to guarantee to *all* men those human freedoms enjoyed by the majority. He also asserted that America must never endorse the idea of slavery as a positive good.

Two days after the inauguration of James Buchanan—who favored allowing slavery in the new territories—the U.S. Supreme Court handed down a decision that profoundly affected the debate over slavery. It involved a slave named Dred Scott. Owned by an army surgeon, Scott had, for a time, been taken from Missouri into Illinois, where slavery was illegal. After the death of his master, Scott, again in Missouri, sued for freedom on the grounds that his prior residence in Illinois had made him free. The case had dragged on for 11 years. Now, in 1857, Chief Justice Roger B. Taney, who was openly sym-

The Republican party (which Lincoln was to join in 1856) was founded in this Ripon, Wisconsin, schoolhouse on February 28, 1854. Primarily a coalition of former Whigs and Democrats who opposed the Kansas-Nebraska Act, the Republicans were committed to keeping slavery out of America's new territories.

Illinois Republicans convene in June 1856 to choose a candidate for the U.S. Senate. Infuriated by the Kansas-Nebraska Act and the Dred Scott decision, they rallied around Lincoln, nominating him to run against Democratic candidate Stephen A. Douglas.

pathetic to the Southern slaveowners, spoke for the Supreme Court: Dred Scott was not free. Blacks were not guaranteed citizenship under the Constitution. Furthermore, the Court ruled, Congress could not prohibit slavery in the new territories. Going beyond even Stephen Douglas's views, the Court decided that the people of a territory could not prohibit slaveholding within that territory's borders.

President Buchanan, the Democrats, and many people throughout the South were jubilant. The Republicans, organized to fight against slavery in the new territories, were furious. The Dred Scott decision, Lincoln believed, directly threatened to upset the balance between North and South, free and slave. In a speech at the Illinois statehouse, Lincoln declared that the Supreme Court ruling was wrong, that the decision must somehow be overturned, and that he would do all in his power to see that this was done.

In June 1856 the Republicans of Illinois assembled in Springfield to select a candidate to run against Stephen Douglas for the U.S. Senate. Unfurled on the convention floor were banners proclaiming: "Every man for Lincoln." Lincoln won easily.

On June 16, 1858, Lincoln delivered the speech that launched his campaign against Douglas. With its short memorable phrases, precise logic, and informal style, the speech attracted the attention of Republican party leaders across the North.

To hold black people in bondage, Lincoln said, was not simply a matter of self-government. It was morally wrong. "A house divided against itself," said Lincoln, quoting from the Bible, "cannot stand." "I believe," he continued, "this government cannot endure, permanently half *slave* and half *free*. I do not expect the Union to be *dissolved*—I do not expect the house to *fall*—but I *do* expect it will cease to be divided."

Missouri-born slave Dred Scott (1795–1858), whose contention that his temporary residence in Illinois, where slavery was illegal, made him free, was rejected by the U.S. Supreme Court in 1857. Chief Justice Roger B. Taney (1777–1864), one of the nine judges who gave opinions in the case, declared that ". . . [blacks] had no rights which the white man was bound to respect."

HON. ABRAHAM LINCOLN, OF ILLINOIS,

HON. HANNIBAL HAMLIN, OF MAINE,

PRESIDENT.

VICE PRESIDENT.

8

Center Stage

The contrast between Abraham Lincoln and Stephen Douglas was striking. One was a tall, raw-boned, self-educated, prairie lawyer who traveled by ordinary passenger train and carried his own bag; the other was a short, stocky, smartly dressed gentleman who rode in a private railroad car and had expensive tastes. One, a relative newcomer to national politics, was the underdog, the unassuming man of humble origins and strong character; the other was the favorite—confident, experienced, and stylish.

The Lincoln-Douglas contest was much more than a race for an Illinois senate seat; it became the focus for the nation's debate over slavery. The self-assured Douglas had run up against an articulate and outspoken opponent, and the campaign seized the attention of the press. Correspondents from the East jockeyed for news stories; telegraph lines carried the words of the candidates to every part of the country. In his "House Divided" speech Lincoln had issued a challenge; Douglas wasted no time in accepting it.

At first, the two did not engage in formal debates on the same platform. Douglas would often appear

Stephen A. Douglas, whom Lincoln debated in 1858, consistently supported the extension of slavery. In one of his replies to Douglas, Lincoln likened slavery to a cancer that could not be removed without the patient bleeding to death, and then declared: ". . . but surely it is no way to cure it, to engraft it and spread it over your whole body."

A Republican party banner for the presidential election of 1860 shows Lincoln and Hannibal Hamlin (1809–1891), the Republican vice-presidential candidate.

at a rally, make a speech, and leave town. A day or two later, Lincoln would make his own speech in the same town, refuting his opponent.

Eventually, the two candidates agreed to seven face-to-face debates. They crisscrossed Illinois to the accompaniment of bands, fireworks, parades, cannon salutes, and peddlers selling Lincoln and Douglas badges. The serious confrontations in which they engaged directly reflected the bitter divisions in the country. Compared to the extremists on both sides—the Southern "fire-eaters," who were ready to protect slavery even at the expense of national unity, and the abolitionists, who were prepared to fight to the death to stamp out what they believed was the nation's greatest moral evil—both Lincoln and Douglas held moderate philosophical positions.

In advocating popular sovereignty, Douglas had said that he did not care "whether slavery be voted *down* or voted *up*," only that the decision be made by a majority vote of the people. Douglas sought to portray Lincoln as a "black Republican," a man who, along with his gang of abolitionist friends, wanted to free millions of slaves who would stampede from the South into the rest of the country, taking white jobs and marrying white daughters. Douglas believed that Lincoln was attempting to impose his own moral judgments on an entire section of the country. Lincoln's misguided meddling, declared Douglas, was threatening to tear the Union apart. Playing on his opponent's antislavery beliefs, Douglas sarcastically mocked what he called "Mr. Lincoln's conscientious belief that the Negro was made his equal, and hence his brother." Douglas declared that the United States government "was made by the white man, for the benefit of the white man, to be administered by white men . . . I do not regard the Negro as my equal. . . ." Douglas presented himself as a trustworthy veteran, a reasonable man dedicated to the well-being of the entire nation, not just to that of a single section.

Douglas's race-baiting forced Lincoln to assume a political stance designed to soothe the racial fears of Illinois citizens and, at the same time, to be consistent with his ultimate goal of preventing the ex-

Our reliance against tyranny is in the love of liberty which God has planted in us. Our defense is in the spirit which prized liberty as the heritage of all men, in all lands everywhere. Destroy this spirit and you have planted the seeds of despotism at your own doors. Familiarize yourselves with the chains of bondage and you prepare your own limbs to wear them. Accustomed to trample on the rights of others, you have lost the genius of your own independence and become the fit subjects of the first cunning tyrant who rises among you.
—ABRAHAM LINCOLN
speech during campaign
against Stephen A. Douglas
for seat in U.S. Senate,
September 1858

pansion of slavery. Lincoln did not advocate the right of blacks to vote, nor did he favor interracial marriage. He said he believed that the "physical difference" between the races would be likely to prevent their living together as social equals. But the black race, Lincoln declared, must be given the right to liberty and equality of opportunity. In having the right to eat the bread of their labor, blacks were, said Lincoln, "my equal and the equal of Judge Douglas, and the equal of every living man." All Lincoln asked for the black man was "that if you do not like him, let him alone. If God gave him but little, that little let him enjoy."

Lincoln argued that Douglas and the Supreme Court were wrong in denying that the Declaration of Independence applied to blacks. The founding fathers, said Lincoln, had held out a noble vision of liberty for all humankind; they had hoped to create a model free society. As a nation, Lincoln declared, the American people should work to extend and enhance "the happiness and value of life to all people of all colors everywhere."

The Illinois election was extremely close. At that time, senators were selected by state legislatures,

With his opponent, Stephen A. Douglas, seated at his right, Lincoln delivers a speech against slavery to the people of an Illinois town in 1858. Following his defeat by Douglas in the Illinois elections for the U.S. Senate, Lincoln remained convinced that during the debates he had made "some marks which will tell for the cause of liberty long after I am gone."

John Brown (1800—1859) became something of a martyr to Northern abolitionists following his execution for leading a raid on a federal armory as part of a plan to establish a nation of fugitive slaves. Poet Ralph Waldo Emerson (1803—1882) called him "that new saint" who "will make the gallows glorious like the cross."

not by direct popular vote. When the final numbers were tallied, the Republicans had not won enough seats in the legislature to send Lincoln to the U.S. Senate.

Lincoln did not regret having competed in the race, but he was deeply disappointed by its outcome. "I feel like the boy who stumped his toe," he told sympathetic friends. "I am too big to cry and too badly hurt to laugh."

Douglas returned to Washington as senator from Illinois. Nevertheless, the debates had hurt his chances of being nominated for the presidency in 1860. Attempting to keep the Democratic party from splitting into Northern and Southern factions, he had insisted that the people of each new state had the right to accept or reject slavery. For this, he was labeled a "traitor to the South," which would now look elsewhere for a spokesman.

Although Lincoln lost the election, the extensive press coverage that the campaign received had elevated him to a position of national prominence. He had demonstrated keen intelligence and great political skill and was now a formidable figure in the Republican party. Some Illinois newspapers even began to suggest that Lincoln should run for the presidency in 1860; others thought him a perfect running mate for the leading figure in the party, William Henry Seward of New York.

During the months following the election, Lincoln continued to make speeches calling for an end to the expansion of slavery. But he also called on reasonable citizens in both the North and the South to exercise moderation and to work toward a peaceful settlement of the slavery controversy.

On October 16, 1859, the moderates suffered a devastating blow. As it had in Kansas, violence over the slavery issue now erupted in Virginia, bringing in its wake more deaths and more cries for revenge. This time the scene was Harper's Ferry, north of Washington, D.C., along the Potomac River. (In 1863 this area would declare itself the separate state of West Virginia.) Some 20 abolitionists, led by a bearded fanatic named John Brown, seized the federal armory as part of a vague plan to establish a nation of fugitive slaves. Brown saw himself as a divine agent sent to rid the land of slavery. The insurrection, in which the mayor of Harper's Ferry was murdered, was short-lived. By the following day, state and federal troops had killed 10 of the conspirators and captured five, including Brown. Convicted of murder and treason, Brown was hanged on December 2.

Brown's insurrection intensified Southerners' fears that the North was inciting blacks to rebellion. Southern newspapers and orators lashed out at the abolitionists, calling them "midnight assassins," and claiming that the abolitionists were being directed by Northern Republicans. Senator Jefferson Davis of Mississippi called the raid "the first . . . of those violent proceedings which can only be considered civil war." The Richmond *Enquirer* now openly predicted that the Southern states would secede from the Union.

In Northern abolitionist circles, John Brown came to be seen as something of a martyr. The poet Ralph Waldo Emerson called him "that new saint" who "will make the gallows glorious like the cross." Senator Henry Wilson of Massachusetts concluded that Brown, "by his bearing, his courage, his words, his acts, has excited the deepest sympathy of many men. . . ." Following Brown's execution, black bunting appeared on windows and church bells tolled throughout the North. Just before he was led to his death, Brown had handed out a written message: the crimes of the land, it declared, would never be purged "but with Blood."

By 1859, the middle ground in the slavery dispute had all but disappeared. Events seemed to be occurring with lightning speed, provoking hysterical cries for retaliation, war, and secession. Those in both the North and the South saw their opponents as forces of evil to be destroyed.

Lincoln continued to tell audiences throughout the North that the Republican party did not support the schemes of John Brown, and had no wish to incite slave uprisings. He argued that the slavery question should be decided just as other constitutional issues are decided—by votes.

Public opinion is everything. With public sentiment nothing can fail. Without it, nothing can succeed. Consequently, he who molds public opinion goes deeper than he who enacts statutes or pronounces decisions.
—ABRAHAM LINCOLN
speaking in Columbus, Ohio,
September 16, 1859

On February 27, 1860, Lincoln delivered a speech to an audience of distinguished New York City Republicans, many of whom had never before heard of the Illinois lawyer. The address, which Lincoln gave at the Cooper Institute, was a spectacular success. One journalist said that never before had a speaker made such an immediate impact on a New York audience. Lincoln advised the Republicans to avoid violence but to refuse to yield to Southern demands on slavery. He urged them to allow no threat, however great, to sway them from their sense of duty. "Let us have faith that right makes might," he said, "and in that faith, let us, to the end, dare to do our duty as we understand it."

The shepherd drives the wolf from the sheep's throat, for which the sheep thanks the shepherd as his liberator, while the wolf denounces him for the same act as the destroyer of liberty, especially as the sheep was a black one. Plainly, the sheep and the wolf are not agreed upon a definition of the word "liberty."
—ABRAHAM LINCOLN

Many Americans realized that the election of 1860 would be a political showdown between the supporters and opponents of slavery. The Democratic party held its national convention in Charleston, South Carolina, in late April, and was quickly engulfed in bitter quarrels. Douglas failed to win back the Southern state leaders, who now completely mistrusted both Douglas and his concept of popular sovereignty. Delegation after delegation of Southerners walked out of the hall. The Democrats reassembled at another convention six weeks later in Baltimore, Maryland. Again, the Southerners walked out, this time for good. The remaining delegates chose Douglas as the Democratic presidential candidate. At a nearby hall in Baltimore, the Southern Democrats chose Vice-President John C. Breckinridge to head a new, pro-slavery party. The Democratic party was now hopelessly split.

Meanwhile, another group, the Constitutional Union party (which was organized by ex-Whig leaders), met to select a presidential candidate and a vice-presidential candidate. The party chose old-line Whigs John Bell of Tennessee and Edward Everett of Boston. The Constitutional Unionists' declared aim was to preserve the Union and the Constitution.

As for the Republicans, U.S. Senator William H. Seward of New York had long been considered the likely choice. But Seward symbolized the uncompromising and militant antislavery faction of the party, and seemed likely to jeopardize its chances in the crucial midwestern and border states. When the Republican leadership looked at other candidates, especially senators Salmon P. Chase of Ohio and Simon Cameron of Pennsylvania, they saw men who had solid reputations as professional politicians, but who were probably even less likely to attract votes.

The Republican leaders then looked to Illinois, which they considered a pivotal state. There they saw a regional politician whose numerous defeats and relative lack of administrative experience in no way detracted from his political stature, which had grown immensely following his sterling performance in his debates with Stephen Douglas. The Republican leaders felt that Lincoln's rural background made him seem more a man of the people than a tool of political machines. Also important was the fact that he had fewer enemies in the party than the other candidates.

In May 1860 the Republicans gathered in Chicago to choose the man to run against Douglas and the

A stylized representation of Lincoln and Stephen A. Douglas in debate. The famed verbal confrontations between the two men took place in 1858. Douglas defended his pro-slavery legislation, while Lincoln contended that slavery should be prohibited in the new territories.

others. Illinois political leaders went all out for their Springfield lawyer. Thousands gathered to show their support for "Honest Abe." After a mad scramble for votes by the candidates' managers, the delegates began to shift, and it became apparent that Lincoln might gain a majority. On the third ballot, Lincoln was victorious. As a cannon boomed from the roof of the building where the convention was being held, a spontaneous parade formed in the streets outside. It all seemed astonishing. At what was perhaps the most crucial point in the country's history, a relative newcomer to the national political stage had emerged as a serious contender for the presidency of the United States.

Despite the momentous nature of the 1860 election, the campaign was filled with the usual carnival atmosphere. Lincoln stayed in Springfield while his lieutenants sharpened his image as a rail-splitting son of the prairie untainted by the grime of politics. Republicans organized rallies with supporters carrying replicas of rails supposedly split by their hero.

Only Douglas brought his message to the country in person. He delivered speeches in city after city in a last-ditch attempt to reunite the Northern and Southern wings of the Democratic party. Even after he realized that he had forfeited the South's support and therefore had no chance of success, Douglas maintained a grueling schedule, imploring the South not to break up the Union even if Lincoln became president. Travel and tension took a terrible toll on Stephen Douglas; he was to die, at age 48, just eight months after the election.

On November 6, 1860, Abraham Lincoln was elected president of the United States. Carrying 18 Northern states, he captured almost 1.9 million votes. Douglas was second in the popular vote with almost 1.4 million. All of the 11 Southern states gave majorities to John Breckinridge. The Constitutional Unionists' candidate, John Bell, received more than half a million votes. The election further demonstrated the grim political divisions wracking the country.

For the South, the election of Lincoln was a call to secession. Despite Lincoln's assurances that the crisis could be settled, and his claim that he would not disturb slavery in the states where it already existed, Southerners regarded his victory as a catastrophe. They considered it the final blow in what they saw as a Northern plot to destroy their way of life.

On December 20, 1860, a state convention in South Carolina declared "that the union now subsisting between South Carolina and the other States, under the name of the 'United States of America' is hereby dissolved." By February 1861, six more states had followed South Carolina's example. The Union had broken apart. The South Carolina *Mercury* proclaimed: "The revolution of 1860 has been initiated."

The day after he was elected, Lincoln had said to the reporters surrounding him, "Well, boys, your troubles are over now; mine have just begun." His words were spoken lightly, but meant seriously. Not even Lincoln, however, could have foreseen how well-founded his fears would prove to have been.

During the presidential election campaign of 1860, many of Lincoln's supporters referred to themselves as "Wide Awakes." Here, a procession of Wide Awakes, bearing flaming torches, marches in New York in October 1860.

9

Preserving the Union

It was a time for reflection and a time for farewells. Lincoln traveled to the remote Illinois village where his aging stepmother, Sally, lived. He spent the day reminiscing with her, calling on old friends, and visiting his father's grave. The next day, at the train station, Sally embraced her beloved stepson for the last time.

Back in Springfield, Lincoln sat alone in a dusty back room above a store on the square, composing his inaugural address. What could he say to a nation perilously close to civil war? How could he assure his countrymen that he would prove equal to the task of leading them in this time of crisis?

Lincoln also spent some time in the law office with his partner, straightening up books, talking over old times and old cases. He requested that the sign "Lincoln and Herndon" be kept in place. The partnership would continue when he returned. Taking a last look at the office, he walked out, grumbling to Herndon about all the appointment-seekers already on his heels. He told his friend how sad he felt to be leaving Springfield, and finally admitted he had a strange feeling he would never return.

President-elect Abraham Lincoln arrives in Washington, D.C., on February 23, 1861. Although civil war was now imminent, Lincoln declared his hope that "[the] mystic chords of memory, stretching from every . . . patriot grave . . . will yet swell the chorus of the Union, when again touched, as surely they will be, by the better angels of our nature."

Jefferson Davis (1808–1889) was inaugurated president of the newly formed Confederate States of America on February 18, 1861, a few months after Lincoln was elected president of the United States.

On February 11, 1861, a cold rain marked the departure of Springfield's most famous son. Lincoln had asked Mary not to accompany him to Washington, fearing that there might, indeed, be some substance to all the hate mail he had received, all the threats, all the rumors of plans to assassinate him. Mary insisted on remaining at her husband's side. They finally agreed that Lincoln and Robert would leave first and that Mary and the younger boys would join them in Indianapolis for the final journey to the White House.

A thousand people had gathered early that morning to see Lincoln off. In the waiting room at the Great Western Railroad depot, he shook hands with friends and neighbors, fellow lawyers and politicians. Outside, the crowd called for a speech. Lincoln mounted the platform of the train and said goodbye: "My friends—No one, not in my situation, can appreciate my feeling of sadness at this parting. To this place, and the kindness of these people, I owe everything. Here I have lived a quarter of a century, and have passed from a young to an old man. Here my children have been born, and one is buried. I now leave, not knowing when, or whether ever, I may return." The train slowly rolled out of the station and headed east.

By this time seven states had quit the Union and begun to make plans to establish a separate government. Some of the South's most able political leaders had gathered in Montgomery, Alabama, to create a new, Southern nation—the Confederate States of America. They had adopted a constitution on February 8, largely patterned after the one Lincoln was now preparing to defend, but with a major additional feature—the central government was prohibited from passing any law denying the right to own slaves. To head their new government, the Montgomery delegates chose Mississippi's Jefferson Davis, former soldier, congressman, senator, and secretary of war. Davis was formally inaugurated as president of the Confederacy on February 18, 1861.

As Southern spokesmen continued their attacks against the evils of "Black Republicanism" and its "diabolical" leader, Abraham Lincoln, the presiden-

Perpetuity is implied, if not expressed, in the fundamental law of all national governments. It is safe to assert that no government proper ever had a provision in its organic law for its own termination.
—ABRAHAM LINCOLN
quoted from his first
inaugural address,
March 4, 1861

tial train crossed Indiana and Ohio and entered Pennsylvania. Lincoln waved to the crowds lining the route and gave short speeches from the train and from hotel balconies. He told his audiences that finding a solution to the problems confronting the country would take both time and patience.

Lincoln seemed genuinely puzzled by the depth and ferocity of the Southerners' hatred. "Why all this excitement?" he asked in Pittsburgh. "Why all these complaints?" He had not threatened to destroy the South's slave system. His had been a voice of moderation. It was now up to the people to rally together to save the Union. But if trouble escalated, if the Union were threatened by radicals and demagogues, he would put his "foot down firmly."

In Philadelphia, Lincoln raised a flag at Independence Hall and talked of the "great principle . . . that kept this nation together. . . . It was that which gave promise that in due time the weights should be lifted from the shoulders of all men, and that all

A Southern planter and his wife stroll in the garden surrounding their palatial residence during the 1850s. In one of his attacks on Southern slaveowners, Lincoln, who considered their belief that the system of slavery could last indefinitely ridiculous, stated: "The [South] has eyes but does not see, and ears but does not hear."

should have an equal chance." The weight on the shoulders of the president-elect was enormous.

When railroad detective Allan Pinkerton told Lincoln that his agents had learned of a serious plot to assassinate him in Baltimore, Lincoln's aides, unsure whether they could provide the president-elect with adequate protection, persuaded Lincoln to change trains, disguise himself, slip through Baltimore at night, and arrive in Washington unannounced. Lincoln was to regret that night for the rest of his life. Southern spokesmen and commentators were quick to attack him, calling him cowardly and unmanly. Cartoons portrayed a frightened Lincoln peering out of a boxcar.

On March 4, 1861, at 12:30 P.M., a carriage carrying James Buchanan, president of the United States, pulled up before the Willard Hotel in Washington. He was there to collect his successor. Buchanan and Lincoln rode down cobblestoned Pennsylvania Avenue to the United States Capitol, where the inaugural ceremonies were to be held. The bright sunshine, the bands, the flags, and the floats masked the uncertainty of this time and this day. All along the parade route, army riflemen were stationed on housetops; cavalry units had taken up positions in the side streets. At the Capitol, its uncompleted dome still surrounded by scaffolding, sharpshooters knelt at the windows.

Standing on the wooden platform that had been erected at the Capitol's east portico, Lincoln adjusted his steel-rimmed eyeglasses and began to speak. His voice, high-pitched but firm, could be heard clearly, even by those at the fringes of the crowd of 25,000. In his carefully crafted inaugural address, Lincoln renewed his pledge not to interfere with slavery in the states where it already existed. He also made it absolutely clear that he was determined to preserve the Union. Lincoln talked of the presidency as a solemn trust whose principal responsibility was to uphold the provisions of the Constitution. He said nothing in the Constitution allowed a state to "lawfully get out of the Union." Any attempt by individual states to secede from the Union was illegal, and any violent acts to support

We [the North and the South] are not enemies, but friends. We must not be enemies. Though passion may have strained, it must not break, our bonds of affection. The mystic chords of memory stretching from every battlefield and patriot grave to every living heart and hearthstone all over this broad land, will yet swell the chorus of the Union when again touched, as surely they will be, by the better angels of our nature.
—ABRAHAM LINCOLN
in his first inaugural address

secession were acts of revolution. "In your hands, my dissatisfied fellow countrymen, and not in mine, is the momentous issue of civil war. The government will not assail you. You can have no conflict, without being yourselves the aggressors. You have no oath registered in Heaven to destroy the government, while I shall have the most solemn one to 'preserve, protect and defend' it."

The political tensions between North and South finally erupted into serious fighting in mid-April 1861, at Fort Sumter, a U.S. Army outpost on an island off Charleston, South Carolina. The 80 soldiers manning the fort were commanded by Major Robert Anderson, of Kentucky. The South Carolinians regarded the continued presence of the U.S. flag flying atop the fort as an affront to their decision to withdraw from the Union. They now considered federal occupancy of Fort Sumter illegal. When Southern leaders demanded that the United States evacuate the fort, Lincoln faced a crisis.

Only two weeks after Lincoln's inauguration, thousands of rebel soldiers surrounded Fort Sumter. For Lincoln to abandon the fort would be a sign of weakness and lack of resolve; to resort to force might precipitate war. All the anxieties of his life, Lincoln said later, were as nothing compared to those that assailed him during the few weeks that followed.

Lincoln worked feverishly to salvage the situation. He consulted with Secretary of State William Seward, Secretary of War Simon Cameron, and Secretary of the Navy Gideon Welles. He talked to secret agents recently returned from the South. He exchanged messages with Major Anderson. Finally, on April 6, Lincoln informed the governor of South Carolina that a fleet was on its way carrying supplies to the beleaguered fort. The federal government, he said, would not be intimidated by threats. The next move was up to the South.

Acting on instructions from Confederate President Davis, the Confederate commander in Charleston, General Pierre Beauregard, demanded the surrender of Fort Sumter. Anderson refused, and at 4:30 A.M. on April 12, 1861, the first shot of the Civil

A Southern newspaper cartoon portrays a frightened Lincoln nervously peering out of a boxcar during his journey to Washington to assume the presidency. Rumors of an assassination plot forced Lincoln to travel in disguise, an action that Southerners construed as a sign of cowardice.

War was fired. Beauregard had ordered Charleston's powerful shore batteries to begin shelling the fort. The voice of reason was no longer audible in the momentous dispute between North and South.

For 34 hours, thousands of Confederate shells screamed through the sky above Charleston and smashed into Fort Sumter. On April 14, afraid his ammunition supplies would ignite and blow the fort apart, Anderson surrendered. He and his men marched out of the fort in full ceremonial order, colors flying and drums beating. Ironically, the battle's only death—the first of the war—occurred when a soldier was killed by a misfiring cartridge during the 50-gun salute that accompanied the surrender.

With the news of the surrender of Fort Sumter, a wave of war hysteria swept the North. This "whirlwind of patriotism," as Massachusetts essayist and poet Ralph Waldo Emerson called it, drove men and women to write songs and poems, design posters,

The first serious fighting of the Civil War erupts as Confederate artillerymen commence the bombardment of Fort Sumter, a U.S. Army outpost on an island off Charleston, South Carolina, on April 12, 1861. Major Robert Anderson (1805–1871) surrendered the fort two days later.

TO ARMS!
RALLY FOR THE RIGHT!
Recruits Wanted
For THREE MONTHS SERVICE, IN
COMPANY A
GRAY RESERVES
CAPT. CHARLES S. SMITH.
ARMORY,
810 MARKET STREET,
UP STAIRS.

Posters calling for Union recruits to fight in the Civil War attracted thousands of eager volunteers following the Confederate victory at Fort Sumter. Lincoln, who had hoped that the dispute between the North and the South might be settled without recourse to violence, now conceded that the Southern rebellion would have to be halted by force.

and stitch countless American flags. Volunteers rushed to the recruiting offices. "Sometimes," Emerson observed, "gunpowder smells good."

Lincoln announced that "combinations too powerful to be suppressed" by the ordinary machinery of government had created an insurrection. The man who, as a presidential candidate, had been confident that war could be avoided, now issued a call for 75,000 volunteers "to cause the laws to be executed."

Although he desperately wanted to preserve the peace, Lincoln regarded the American experiment in democracy as worth defending at all costs. He saw the Southern rebellion as a challenge to the nation's history, as an affront to its founding fathers, and as an assault upon the ideals to which those men had been dedicated. Lincoln was determined to see the Southern rebellion crushed.

LINCOLN'S TWO DIFFICULTIES.

Lin. "WHAT? NO MONEY! NO MEN!"

10

Blue and Gray

A foot-stamping, screaming crowd of 50,000 jammed New York's Union Square on April 20, 1861. They were cheering a speaker who urged them "to rally round the star-bangled banner so long as a single stripe can be discovered, or a single star shall shimmer from the surrounding darkness."

In the South, young men rallied around their own flag, "the Stars and Bars" of the Confederacy, as they sang: "We are a band of brothers / And native to the soil / Fighting for our liberty / With treasure, blood and toil. . . ."

The call to war was almost a relief. The talking and compromising were over, suspense lifted, passions unleashed, patriotism renewed. Massachusetts novelist Nathaniel Hawthorne described what he felt as a spirit of heroism and love of country, a spirit that made him feel young again.

Men and boys were about to kill and be killed. Families, divided in their loyalties, would soon break apart. The country's political system was in chaos. More important to Americans in 1861 were their colors—the Union's blue, the Confederacy's gray. This was a time of causes for which to fight, beliefs for which to die.

At the beginning of the Civil War, Massachusetts novelist Nathaniel Hawthorne (1804–1864), author of *The Scarlet Letter* and *The House of the Seven Gables*, thought the prospect of conflict somewhat romantic and believed that there was a new spirit of patriotism abroad in the North.

A British cartoon satirizes the desperate situation that had come to beset Lincoln by 1862—the second year of the Civil War. Lacking both money and men, Lincoln began to contemplate freeing the slaves and ordering the induction of black males into the Union forces.

One of the war's early casualties was a beloved young friend of the Lincoln family, Colonel Elmer Ellsworth, who was shot dead while hauling down a Confederate flag in Alexandria, Virginia. "So much of promised usefulness to one's country, and of bright hopes for one's self and friends, have rarely been so suddenly dashed," wrote Lincoln to Ellsworth's parents. Lincoln would be writing many such letters in the coming months and years, letters that would weigh more and more heavily on his spirit as the death toll rose.

When the Civil War began, the North had a considerable advantage in numbers. The 23 Union states had a population of 22 million; the 11 Confederate states, (including Virginia, North Carolina, Tennessee, and Arkansas, which joined the Confederate cause after Lincoln's call to arms) had 9 million people, of whom over 3 million were slaves. The North had a more advanced agricultural system, more heavy industry, more railroads, and more money. The Union navy was vastly superior to that of the Confederates.

> *If I were to try to read, much less answer, all the attacks made on me, this shop might as well be closed for any other business.*
> —ABRAHAM LINCOLN

The South, however, possessed certain tactical and psychological advantages. Its troops would be fighting a defensive war, mostly on their own, familiar land. Its citizens were fiercely loyal and its officer corps, led by General Robert E. Lee of Virginia, was superb.

Lee, who was descended from one of Virginia's most illustrious families, was an extraordinary soldier. Lincoln had offered him command of the Union armies, but, loyal to his native state, Lee had refused. Thus, the South now had on its side the country's most able military leader.

As the two sides rushed to expand their forces, Lincoln and the federal government found themselves in an extremely vulnerable position. Peering through a spyglass from his White House window, Lincoln could see the Confederate flag flying across the Potomac River, just a few miles from where he stood. The Virginians were boasting that the Stars and Bars would be flying over the nation's capital before May. To the north, the state of Maryland vacillated between loyalty to the Union and sympathy with the Confederacy. Near Baltimore, Southern loyalists cut telegraph wires and burned bridges. When the first Northern regiment en route to Washington—the Sixth Massachusetts—marched through Baltimore, a mob of rebel sympathizers attacked them with stones and bullets. Four soldiers and nine civilians died. Washington itself was teeming with Confederate spies and plagued by rumors of plots. Accordingly, Lincoln ordered a 10,000-man defending force into the city. The White House, from which the nation was governed, had now become a fortress.

Neither the North nor the South was prepared for a protracted conflict. Their armies, composed mostly of volunteers, were inexperienced and poorly trained. While ragged troops drilled on thousands of fields across the country, the politicians desperately tried to supply them with sufficient equipment—muskets and cannon, tents and uniforms, ammunition and food. By summer, the ranks of the opposing armies had swelled, and both governments were under pressure from their citizens to attack. Demanding that the Union army conquer the Confederate capital, Horace Greeley's influential and widely read *New York Tribune* was trumpeting the battle cry, "Forward to Richmond!" Southern generals itched to show their tactical superiority in the field and the fighting spirit of their men.

On July 21, 1861, the nation got the war so many seemed to want. It began at Bull Run, a muddy, winding stream near Manassas Junction, Virginia, about 30 miles southeast of Washington. General Winfield Scott, the 75-year-old commander of the U.S. Army, ordered General Irvin McDowell's Union troops to seize the junction from Beauregard's 24,000 Confederate troops. McDowell led his 30,000 brightly dressed men through the rolling cornfields and wooded hills of northern Virginia. Many of the soldiers picked blackberries along the way. It seemed to some of the troops more like a picnic than a war. Indeed, to many civilians it *was* a picnic. As the two armies approached each other around Bull Run, hundreds of Washington civilians, including dozens of congressmen and senators, appeared on

One of the most brilliant generals of his day, Robert E. Lee (1807–1880) resigned from the U.S. Army in 1861, when his home state, Virginia, joined the Confederacy. Lincoln had proposed putting Lee in command of the Union armies, but Lee refused the president's offer.

the scene. Arriving by carriage, by wagon, and on horseback, they came armed with hampers of food and flasks of wine and whiskey. They sat down on the gentle slopes a short distance to the east of where the fighting was expected to take place, and waited for the battle to begin. Some of the spectators were even carrying opera glasses.

The holiday atmosphere evaporated soon after the battle began. Washington society found itself with a grandstand view of its own forces being massacred. The Union army, which had been confident that it could demolish the smaller Confederate force, was stopped in its tracks by the "stonewall" resistance of the Southern troops, who were commanded by General Thomas J. Jackson, known ever afterward as Stonewall Jackson. It was at Bull Run that federal troops first heard the blood-chilling "rebel yell," which inspired fanatical courage in those who uttered it and terror in those against whom it was directed.

At Bull Run, the forces of both sides were inexperienced and undisciplined. Often unsure which troops were their own and which the enemy's, they smashed together in a deadly embrace, fighting bayonet to bayonet. One Confederate soldier later gave a grim account of the dead, describing how their "countenances and postures generally indicated the suffering of agonizing pain."

The Union soldiers, outflanked by the Confederates and weary from the long march from Washington, began to retreat; retreat soon turned to panic. As the Union troops withdrew to Washington with their wagons, artillery, and ambulances, they ran into hundreds of civilians who, horrified by the grim reality of war, were desperately seeking safety. Engulfed in dust and smoke, citizens and soldiers, horses and vehicles madly pushed and shoved. Thousands of bewildered troops dropped their weapons and began to run.

The Confederates did not pursue their defeated opponents. In fact, they seemed almost as disorganized and battered as their enemies. The casualty lists later told the grim story. The federal forces suffered almost 3,000 killed, wounded, or missing at

You know better than any man living that from my boyhood up my ambition was to be President.
—ABRAHAM LINCOLN
speaking to William Herndon
after becoming president

Bull Run; the Confederates nearly 2,000. (The engagement was—and still is—known in the South as the Battle of Manassas. The Union forces usually named battles for the nearest body of water, the Confederates for the nearest town.) Those who had taken a romantic view of war prior to Bull Run now no longer did so. From his window in the White House, Lincoln watched his beaten army limping into Washington through the early morning fog and rain. He had been awake all night, brooding about this insane misery of war. Poet Walt Whitman called it Abraham Lincoln's "crucifixion day."

The president's family (clockwise from left): Lincoln, William, Robert, and Tad. In 1862 11-year-old William died, bringing yet another tragedy to the Lincoln household. Another son, Edward, had died 12 years earlier.

Union and Confederate forces clash in the first major confrontation of the Civil War—the Battle of Bull Run—on July 21, 1861. The Union army was cut to pieces by a Confederate army under the command of General Thomas J. Jackson (1824–1863), whose unflinching resistance against the Union onslaught earned him the nickname "Stonewall."

Bull Run deepened Lincoln's resolve to defeat the Confederacy. He would enlarge the army and improve its discipline and fighting efficiency. He would give serious consideration to General Scott's "anaconda" strategy, which called for squeezing the Confederacy to death by blockading it from the ocean and splitting it along the Mississippi River. Three expeditions would be dispatched simultaneously—into Virginia, into East Tennessee, and down the Mississippi. Lincoln realized that he would do well to appoint more competent generals and advisers.

The first of Lincoln's new appointees was George B. McClellan, a 34-year-old Northern Democrat from Philadelphia. The highly educated McClellan was a skilled military organizer who had graduated from

West Point and served with distinction in the Mexican War. In late 1861, Lincoln named McClellan general in chief of all the armies of the United States, replacing the elderly and ailing Scott. The dashing young McClellan quickly went to work shoring up Washington's defenses and mobilizing the Army of the Potomac.

McClellan, who was handsome, vain, and elegant, considered Lincoln shallow and uncouth. Strutting around Washington reviewing his troops, McClellan soon became something of a folk hero. Many people (including McClellan himself), thought he, not Lincoln, should be in charge of the country. Although Lincoln's friends were outraged by the rudeness and condescension that characterized McClellan's behavior toward the president, Lincoln, as always, was patient, showing much more interest in efficiency than in etiquette. "Never mind," the president said to his angry colleagues, "I will hold McClellan's horse if he will bring us success." Despite his arrogance, McClellan did bring order to the army. By November, he had enlisted nearly 200,000 men in Washington and Virginia. Lincoln waited for him to march on the South. McClellan declared that he needed more time.

During this period, Lincoln named a new secretary of war to replace the ineffectual Simon Cameron. He chose Edwin Stanton, a Democrat, who had little use for Republicans, especially Lincoln, but who was tough, competent, and a strong supporter of the Union. Stanton immediately pressured McClellan to get the federal forces marching. McClellan, however, continued to maintain that he needed more time.

Many Republicans in Congress were growing impatient. They demanded to know when the administration and the army intended to make a move. Congress appointed a "Committee on the Conduct of the War," headed by Senator Benjamin Wade of Ohio. Wade was no admirer of Lincoln's administration, which he privately considered "blundering, cowardly, and inefficient." The committee questioned witnesses who gave secret testimony on the war's progress, or lack of it.

My paramount object in this struggle is to save the Union, and is not either to save or to destroy slavery. If I could save the Union without freeing any slave, I would do it; and if I could save it by freeing all the slaves, I would do it; and if I could do it by freeing some and leaving others alone, I would also do that.
—ABRAHAM LINCOLN
in a letter to Horace Greeley, editor and publisher of the *New York Tribune*, August 22, 1862

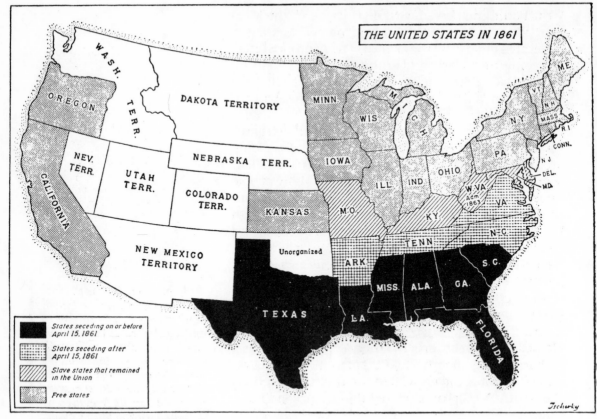

THE UNITED STATES IN 1861

Legend:
- States seceding on or before April 15, 1861
- States seceding after April 15, 1861
- Slave states that remained in the Union
- Free states

Tschurky

A map shows the political division of America following the formation of the Confederacy.

For Lincoln, the war had become a nightmare that haunted him almost perpetually. Thrust into the center of an awesome national conflict, beset by administrative difficulties, Lincoln often seemed literally lost in thought.

Early in 1862, Lincoln's nightmare deepened, this time due to another personal tragedy. Eleven-year-old Willie Lincoln had, like his brother Tad (Thomas), been ill for several days with a slight fever. The White House doctor had been reassuring, but Willie's temperature suddenly shot up, and he began to have chills. His parents could do nothing but watch and wait. The boy died at last on February 20. Lincoln was crushed by the loss of this bright, gentle boy he had loved so deeply. Mary was distraught with grief. Sobbing uncontrollably, she stayed in her room for three months. She eventually found solace in visiting hospitals and distributing food to wounded soldiers. But she was now a woman haunted by fear and sorrow.

Lincoln confessed to a friend that he was "not at all hopeful" about his own or his country's fate. Dispirited as he was, however, he saw the war in a broader perspective than did those around him. He still believed that out of the chaos and blood must come the preservation of America's bold experiment in democracy and its commitment to human liberty. He would now take firm control, directing the day-to-day conduct of the war. He was determined to see the conflict through to a right and just conclusion.

Lincoln realized that the Union cause was threatened by opposition to the war within the nation. The war's main opponents were Southern sympa-

Like this young Confederate soldier, many recruits on both sides in the Civil War were boys who could barely handle a rifle. Although commanded by capable officers, the armies of both the North and the South were largely composed of inexperienced volunteers.

Union General Ulysses S. Grant (1822–1885), who was known as "Unconditional Surrender" Grant, came under much criticism when his forces suffered staggering losses following a surprise Confederate attack at Shiloh, in southwestern Tennessee, in April 1862. Lincoln refused to have him replaced, declaring: "I can't spare this man. He fights."

thizers and the large number of Democrats—nick-named Copperheads—who wanted to call a truce with the South and amend the Constitution to guarantee states rights, including the right to practice slavery.

Lincoln began to exercise harsh war policies. The most unpopular of these was the imposition of martial (military) law, which he proclaimed in 1862. He suspended the right of *habeas corpus*, which meant the army could seize and hold alleged traitors without trial. More than 13,000 people were arrested and jailed under this proclamation. Lincoln, who had attacked President Polk for his unconstitutional use of presidential power during the Mexican War, was now exercising more arbitrary power than any of his predecessors. He expected to be charged with abusing his authority, but saw these as extraordinary times that demanded extraordinary measures.

Early in 1862, the Northern forces began a broad offensive in the West. Against the armies led by Confederate General Albert Sidney Johnston, the Union gained key victories at Pea Ridge, New Madrid, and "Island No. 10" in southeastern Missouri; at Mill Springs in Kentucky; and at Fort Henry, on the Tennessee River. The Union armies were also victorious at Fort Donelson, on the Cumberland River in northwestern Tennessee. There, under the command of General Ulysses S. Grant, the Union army relentlessly pounded 20,000 hard-fighting Confederate troops. On February 16, 1862, the commander of the Confederate forces at Fort Donelson finally met Grant's demand: "No terms but immediate and unconditional surrender." The general's words—and his initials—gained him a lifelong nickname: "Unconditional Surrender" Grant; his actions made him a national hero.

Early in April, Grant's troops stood fast against a surprise Confederate onslaught at Shiloh, in southwestern Tennessee. The battle was the largest in the nation's history up to that time. The scene at Shiloh was one of unparalleled horror. About 24,000 soldiers, many of them boys who hardly knew how to handle a rifle, were killed or injured. One private remarked that Shiloh was "one, never-ending, terrible roar." Among the Confederate dead was General Johnston. Grant's losses and his unpreparedness provoked a storm of criticism in Washington, and Lincoln was urged to replace him. The president refused. "I can't spare this man," he said. "He fights."

Further south, in Louisiana, the great Mississippi River port of New Orleans surrendered to the Union fleet of Captain David G. Farragut; and other key Southern cities, including Baton Rouge, Louisiana, also capitulated. The Union campaign in the West was achieving considerable success.

The focus of national attention, however, was on the situation in the East. Could McClellan's Army of the Potomac at last go "forward to Richmond?" The main Union force of 110,000 men was finally floated down the Potomac River from Washington aboard transport vessels. On April 4, 1862, the Union force disembarked on the York peninsula, 75 miles southeast of Richmond. From there, McClellan, who was convinced that the Confederates had a large force defending the Southern capital, slowly and methodically moved northward. McClellan did not realize that the rebel army was, in fact, badly outnumbered. The Union plan was to send some 30,000 troops from the north to meet McClellan's troops at Richmond, thus pinching the enemy in a vise. The combined force would have had an overwhelming advantage against Lee's actual army of 85,000. The Confederates, however, managed to outmaneuver the Army of the Potomac. Between May 4 and June 9 of 1862, Stonewall Jackson conducted harassing raids throughout northern Virginia, gaining several stunning victories over the Union armies. Jackson's successes convinced the Northerners that the Confederacy was planning a major assault against Washington. As a result, the reinforcements for which McClellan had been waiting never arrived. Instead, they were recalled to Washington to defend the capital against the anticipated attack. Weeks of bloody but inconclusive fighting followed. By August, McClellan was no closer to taking Richmond than he had been in April. The war would go on.

General Thomas J. Jackson, who helped lead the Confederate army to a number of victories during the first two years of the Civil War, was accidentally killed by one of his own troops in 1863.

11

Slavery's Death

Abraham Lincoln and his government did not wage war against the Confederacy to destroy slavery. "My paramount object in this struggle," Lincoln wrote in 1862, "is to save the Union." He hoped that, once the war was over and the nation reunited under its legitimate government, he would be able to establish a program of gradual emancipation of slaves. The federal government would compensate the slaveowners for loss of their "property."

Early in the war Lincoln resisted the demands of the radical faction in Congress, which insisted on the abolition of slavery and the use of black troops in the army. He did so because he feared that Maryland, Delaware, Kentucky, and Missouri—which were all slave states that had remained loyal to the Union—would rebel. He also feared that many Northern moderates were intellectually and emotionally unprepared for such radical change and that they would desert the Union if emancipation legislation were passed. Racial prejudice was, after all, rampant in the North.

As the war intensified, the fate of the North seemed still in the balance, and Lincoln and several

Born a slave, Frederick Douglass (1817–1895) became an abolitionist, journalist, orator, and public official. He urged Lincoln to punish the South "for the attempt to abolish the government" by abolishing slavery. Douglass organized black troops to fight in the war.

Flanked by General John McClernand (right; 1826–1885) and detective Allan Pinkerton (1819–1884), Lincoln visits Antietam Creek in Maryland in September 1862. The stunning victory Union forces had gained there shortly before the president's visit convinced Lincoln that absolute victory was now within sight.

of his colleagues began to consider using free blacks and former slaves as soldiers. From the very outset of the conflict, escaped slaves had made seeking refuge with Union army units the first step of their flight to freedom. Some officers had begun to put such runaways to work by declaring them captured property. Escaped slaves were working for the Union forces as teamsters, cooks, and laborers.

By mid-1862, with the war in a stalemate, Lincoln began to look for ways to turn the situation around. "We must change our tactics or lose the war," he declared. He had listened to senators Zachariah Chandler and Benjamin Wade insist that the war be made a death warrant for slavery. He had listened to Senator Charles Sumner's argument that Great Britain, which was now considering whether to recognize the Confederacy as an independent nation, might instead rally behind the Union if it made the abolition of slavery one of its central war aims. Sumner had also drawn Lincoln's attention to what was perhaps the most practical aspect of the need for emancipation and the induction of slaves into the Union forces. "You need more men," Sumner had told him.

Finally, Lincoln had listened to Frederick Douglass, the leading spokesman of the blacks, who had argued that the "Negro is the key to the situation—the pivot upon which the whole rebellion turns. . . . Teach the rebels and traitors that the price they are to pay for the attempt to abolish this government must be the abolition of slavery."

Lincoln was bombarded by petitions, newspaper editorials, speeches, and visitors to the White House, all urging him to free the slaves. Still, he remained hesitant. An emancipation proclamation issued now, he believed, would appear to be the desperate act of a government intent on saving itself by encouraging a slave insurrection within the territories controlled by its opponents. Lincoln waited for the right moment, a moment of victory on the battlefield, when the act of freeing the slaves would seem, not an act of desperation, but one of justice.

That moment came in the fall of 1862. Lee had moved his troops across the Potomac River in a ma-

Fellow citizens, we cannot escape history. We of this Congress and this Administration will be remembered in spite of ourselves. No personal significance or insignificance can spare one or another of us. The fiery trial through which we pass will light us down, in honor or dishonor, to the latest generation.
—ABRAHAM LINCOLN
quoted from his annual
message to Congress,
December 1, 1862

jor thrust toward the North. On September 17, 1862, the Confederates suffered disastrous losses in a ferocious battle with McClellan's forces at Antietam Creek in Maryland. Both armies suffered over 12,000 casualties, but since Lee retired from the battlefield, the engagement was regarded as a federal victory.

Five days after Antietam, Lincoln issued a preliminary emancipation proclamation, announcing that on January 1, 1863, "all persons held as slaves" in any state still in rebellion against the Union would be "then, thenceforward, and forever free." Although the proclamation did not actually free a single slave—since it applied only to rebel states, where

The offices of slave merchants Price, Birch & Co., in Alexandria, Virginia, c. 1860. Although the abolition of slavery eventually became a major element of the North's war aims, it was the preservation of the Union that was of paramount importance to Lincoln and his supporters.

it could not be enforced—it became one of the most famous public documents in American history. "If my name ever goes into history," Lincoln said, "it will be for this act."

After Lincoln officially signed the proclamation on New Year's Day, 1863, hundreds of cheering people gathered in front of the White House. The president came to the window and bowed. One black man said that if Lincoln came out of "that palace, they would

And by virtue of the power and for the purpose aforesaid, I do order and declare that all persons held as slaves within said designated states and parts of states are, and henceforward shall be, free; and that the executive government of the United States, including the military and naval authorities thereof, will recognize and maintain the freedom of said persons.
—ABRAHAM LINCOLN
in the Emancipation Proclamation, signed January 1, 1863

hug him to death." Douglass was moved to write: "We shout for joy that we live to record this righteous decree." A black preacher said: "The time has come in the history of this nation when the downtrodden and abject black man can assert his rights, and feel his manhood."

As large areas of the South were returned to federal control, their black populations flocked to the Union side. At first, they were used chiefly as la-

A painting shows Lincoln flanked by cabinet members as he reads the first draft of the Emancipation Proclamation in September 1862. Pressured by Congress, the press, and abolitionists throughout the North, Lincoln had finally agreed to bring an end to slavery.

By the President of the United States of America:

A Proclamation.

Whereas, on the twenty-second day of September, in the year of our Lord one thousand eight hundred and sixty-two, a proclamation was issued by the President of the United States, containing, among other things, the following, to wit:

"That on the first day of January, in the year of our Lord one thousand eight hundred and sixty-three, all persons held as slaves within any State or designated part of a State, the people whereof shall then be in rebellion against the United States, shall be then, thenceforward, and forever free; and the Executive Government of the United States, including the military and naval authority thereof, will recognize and maintain the freedom of such persons, and will do no act or acts to repress such persons, or any of them, in any efforts they may make for their actual freedom.

"That the Executive will, on the first

The Emancipation Proclamation—freeing slaves in all states, including those in rebellion—was signed by Lincoln on January 1, 1863. Although blacks in Confederate states were not actually freed at that time, the proclamation gave them new hope by changing the nature of the war.

borers. Many complained bitterly, arguing that they should be given muskets, not axes. Gradually, the army changed its policy and began to arm black troops and send them into combat. By the end of the war, nearly 200,000 former slaves had served in the Union forces as soldiers, sailors, and laborers.

The effect of the Emancipation Proclamation and black military service reverberated throughout the country's black communities, raising the spirits of a people long downtrodden and brutalized. Blacks were now direct participants in the struggle for their liberty. From Mississippi to Massachusetts, blacks now had new hopes and expectations.

Although many white Northern soldiers remained suspicious and contemptuous of their new allies, some of them experienced a great change of heart. One white Philadelphian observed: "In every respect there is not only no repugnance on the part of white soldiers to colored soldiers but a positive disposition to fraternize with them." A black regiment in Tennessee, it was reported, "received three hearty cheers from a regiment of white men" after fighting bravely in battle.

In his annual message to Congress in December 1862, Lincoln had written: "In giving freedom to the slave, we assure freedom to the free—honorable alike in what we give, and what we preserve." The Emancipation Proclamation changed the character of the war. The federal government had inflicted a terrible blow against what had once seemed likely

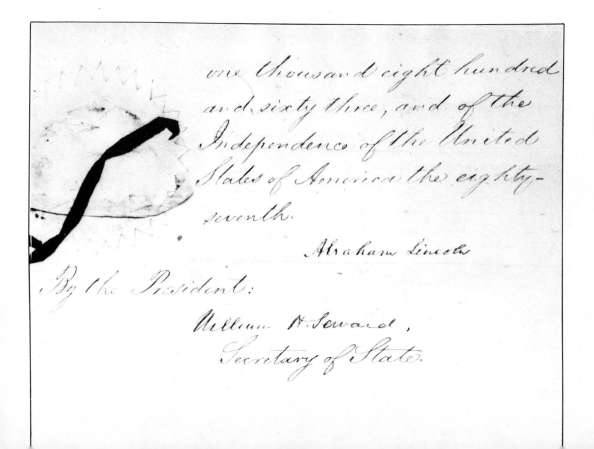

More than a century after the Civil War, black civil rights leader Martin Luther King, Jr. (1929–1968), who was assassinated by a white supremacist, declared that he regarded Lincoln's Emancipation Proclamation to have been "a truly momentous decree."

to remain a permanent institution. As black civil rights leader Martin Luther King, Jr., described it a century later, it was a "momentous decree."

What the Emancipation Proclamation meant to millions of blacks in Lincoln's day, and what it was to mean to later generations, was summed up by Hannah Johnson, a black woman from Buffalo, New York, whose son fought for the Union. Still fearing that somehow the "Freedom Bill" would be taken away, that liberty for her race was only fleeting, she wrote to Lincoln: "They tell me some do that you will take back the Proclamation, don't do it. When you are dead and in Heaven, in a thousand years that action of yours will make the Angels sing your praise. I know it. Ought one man to own another . . . it is wicked, and a horrible outrage, there is no sense in it. . . ."

Private Hubbard Pryor, of the U.S. Colored Division, is pictured here before and after his recruitment in 1864. Former slaves who flocked to the Union side following the Emancipation Proclamation were placed in separate regiments. About 38,000 blacks died in the war.

12

Endless War

As the war continued, Lincoln kept searching for generals who could act decisively and forcefully. He was frustrated and exasperated by McClellan's timidity in the field. After McClellan's failure to take Richmond in 1862, Lincoln had brought in Henry Halleck as general in chief. One of Halleck's first moves had been to put the stern and charismatic General John Pope in command of the Army of the Potomac. Unfortunately, however, the air of authority with which Pope liked to surround himself soon turned out to have been little more than an affectation. His ineffectiveness as an officer became apparent both to his colleagues and to Lincoln. After his appointment to the Army of the Potomac, Pope grandly announced to the press, "My headquarters will be in the saddle!" "A better place," observed Lincoln wryly, "for his hindquarters."

Pope soon suffered a reverse more humiliating than any of the several that had befallen McClellan. In August 1862 he was soundly defeated by Lee at the Second Battle of Bull Run (known to the South as "Second Manassas").

The president had again turned to McClellan, who did manage to stop Lee's advance into Maryland at

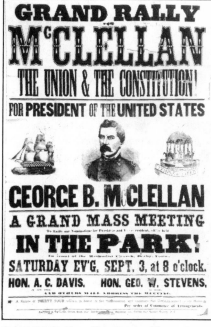

GRAND RALLY
McCLELLAN
THE UNION & THE CONSTITUTION!
FOR PRESIDENT OF THE UNITED STATES

GEORGE B. McCLELLAN
A GRAND MASS MEETING
IN THE PARK!
SATURDAY EV'G, SEPT. 3, at 8 o'clock.
HON. A. C. DAVIS.   HON. GEO. W. STEVENS.

By 1864 the mounting death toll in the Civil War had come to weigh heavily on Lincoln and seemed likely to destroy his chances of reelection. However, following a string of major Union victories in Georgia and Alabama early in the fall of that same year, Lincoln regained the electorate's confidence and soundly defeated his opponent, George B. McClellan (1826–1885), in the presidential election.

In 1864 the Democratic presidential candidate, George B. McClellan, promised that he would, if elected, negotiate an end to the war and restore the Union while leaving the institution of slavery intact.

General William Tecumseh Sherman (1820–1891) led the Union advance into Georgia in 1864, capturing the key Confederate city of Atlanta and then marching on to the port of Savannah, leaving immense devastation and destruction in his wake.

Antietam. However, by failing to give pursuit and thus allowing the Confederates to slip back across the Potomac River into Virginia, McClellan robbed himself of a substantive victory. Lincoln, bewildered by what he called McClellan's "slows," relieved him of his command in November 1862. McClellan's replacement was Ambrose E. Burnside, a personable West Pointer whose military ability was soon revealed to be tragically deficient. Burnside attacked Lee's Army of Northern Virginia at Fredericksburg, Virginia, on December 13. As Burnside's troops built pontoon bridges across the Rappahannock River, Confederate sharpshooters picked them off by the thousands. After he had lost 12,000 men, Burnside withdrew; at his own request he was dismissed from his command.

Lincoln then turned to General Joseph Hooker, a dashing and talented organizer whose confidence bordered on arrogance. In April 1863 Hooker led the Union troops in another drive toward Richmond. "My plans are perfect," he announced, "and when I start to carry them out, may God have mercy on General Lee, for I will have none." But, like his predecessors, the flamboyant "Fighting Joe" was forced into an embarrassing retreat. Lee's army, which was half the size of Hooker's, cut the Union forces to pieces at Chancellorsville, Virginia, in May 1863. Lee paid a high price for his victory. He lost 12,000 men, including his most trusted subordinate, the brilliant Stonewall Jackson.

Chancellorsville convinced Lee that the time was now right for another thrust into the North. A Southern victory on Northern territory might, thought Lee, enable the Confederacy to capture a major city such as Philadelphia, Baltimore, even Washington. Such a victory might even persuade Great Britain to recognize the Confederate government. It might even force Lincoln to negotiate for peace on Confederate terms.

Again, Lee crossed the Potomac, leading the Army of Northern Virginia into Pennsylvania. Hooker had been relieved, and the Army of the Potomac was now commanded by General George G. Meade, a capable, short-tempered, and highly professional soldier who had been seriously wounded during McClellan's attempt to take Richmond. Meade had just assumed his new post when he was faced with one of the pivotal battles of the war—Gettysburg.

Neither Lee nor Meade had planned to fight at this small town in Pennsylvania. Lee, whose army was in constant need of shoes, had sent a foraging party to Gettysburg, where there was said to be a great supply of footwear. On June 30, 1863, the Confederate soldiers encountered a Union cavalry brigade just outside the town. The opposing contingents were so eager for action that they began to fight immediately. On July 1 the battle began in earnest, growing larger as additional units from both armies arrived on the scene. In the next three days, Cemetery Ridge, Culp's Hill, Little Round Top, and Seminary Ridge became the scene of one of the most famous battles ever fought. The terrible struggle between the 75,000-man Army of Northern Virginia and the 88,000-man Army of the Potomac continued until July 3, when Confederate General George E. Pickett led 15,000 men in an assault on Cemetery Ridge, the Union army's high-ground stronghold. Pickett's Charge, as the doomed attack is known to history, resulted in the loss of more than half his troops. The Confederates were forced to withdraw.

Lee led his army, defeated but not destroyed, in an orderly retreat to Sharpsburg, where he was stopped by the flooded Potomac River. Lincoln, following the battle and its aftermath by telegraph, cabled an urgent message to the front: "Do not let the enemy escape." Meade, however, delayed further action, and when the Potomac subsided, Lee led his army back into Virginia. When Meade informed the president that his men had driven "from our soil every vestige of the presence of the invader," Lincoln exclaimed, "My god! Is that all?" Meade should have annihilated Lee's army, not merely driven it back into Virginia. The war was still on.

When news of Lee's escape reached Lincoln, the president despaired. The news from the West, however, was sensational. Ulysses S. Grant—the one man, it seemed, upon whom Lincoln could count to deliver unqualified victories—had taken Vicksburg,

> *I do not allow myself to suppose that either the convention or the League have concluded to decide that I am either the greatest or best man in America, but rather they have concluded that it is not best to swap horses while crossing the river, and have further concluded that I am not so poor a horse that they might not make a botch of it in trying to swap.*
> —ABRAHAM LINCOLN
> replying to his nomination
> as the presidential candidate
> of the National Union League,
> June 9, 1864

Mississippi, on July 4. The Confederacy's only remaining railroad leading east from the Mississippi River was thus lost, giving the Union control over the entire Mississippi Valley. After Grant's subsequent success at Chattanooga later in 1863, Lincoln believed he had found the man to end the war. Early in 1864, he summoned Grant to Washington and appointed him general in chief of all the Union armies.

The 42-year-old Grant, who was about five feet, eight inches tall, was a stoop-shouldered, cigar-smoking, hard-drinking Ohioan. A product of West Point (where he had graduated near the bottom of his class), Grant had served with distinction in the Mexican War, but had been accused of drunkenness and forced to retire from the army in 1854. From that point until he returned to the service in 1861, he had tried unsuccessfully to be a farmer and a real-estate broker, finally spending four years as a clerk in his father's store. Grant, in short, was an unlikely American hero. His image had been much improved following his capture of Fort Donelson in 1862, but he was still widely criticized for his alleged misuse of liquor. (When Lincoln was told that Grant drank whiskey while serving in the field, the president is reported to have said: "Find out the name of his brand so I can give it to my other generals.") Grant may have had what some people considered personal shortcomings, but his brilliance as a military leader was beyond dispute. He and Lincoln soon met for the first time. They liked and respected each other at once.

Lincoln and Grant immediately set about devising a strategy to win the war. Their plan called for a simultaneous attack on the two major Confederate armies—Lee's newly rebuilt Army of Northern Virginia and General Joseph Johnston's Army of Tennessee, each comprising about 60,000 men.

In the East, the fight would be Grant's. Using Meade as commander of the army and General Philip Sheridan as head of the cavalry corps, Grant would remain in the field, overseeing the destruction of Lee's forces.

In the West, General William Tecumseh Sherman

It is called the Army of the Potomac but is only [Union General George B.] McClellan's bodyguard. If McClellan is not using the army, I should like to borrow it for a while.
—ABRAHAM LINCOLN

was to lead the 100,000 men of three Union armies into Georgia to destroy "Old Joe" Johnston's army and take control of the city of Atlanta and its crucial railroads.

In May 1864 the Union launched its two mightiest offensives of the war. Grant led his 115,000-man army across the Rapidan River in Virginia and confronted Lee in the densely forested area known as the Wilderness. As Lincoln waited anxiously in Washington, communicating with Grant by telegraph and tracing his movements on a large map of Virginia in the War Department, his commander in chief inched his troops forward, taking staggering losses. Unlike McClellan and the others, Grant kept going. "I propose to fight it out on this line if it takes all summer," he wired to Lincoln. Every day, steamers unloaded their grim cargo of Union dead and wounded on Washington's wharves. In the Wilderness, injured men bled to death between the lines. Rotting corpses littered the battlefield. In Georgia, Sherman was also meeting stiff resistance and taking heavy casualties. Throughout the North, newspapers, politicians, and private citizens condemned the slaughter, which was rapidly coming to seem senseless and unjustifiable. Neither Grant nor Sherman, despite their remorseless pounding of the enemy, had broken through.

On the political front, Lincoln's chances of being nominated for a second term were jeopardized by the military stalemate, the war's terrible death toll, and the mounting protest in the North. In June 1864, however, he was renominated for the presidency by a National Union convention representing both Republicans and "war Democrats." Lincoln declared that the war must finally end slavery, that a constitutional amendment to emancipate the slaves would be "a fitting and necessary conclusion to the final success of the union cause." Lincoln realized that his Emancipation Proclamation, an executive order made in wartime, could be overturned by a later president. An amendment to the constitution, however, would be permanent. The convention named Andrew Johnson of Tennessee, a loyal Unionist who had refused to follow his state into

> *Abraham Lincoln was the last President of the United States who could genuinely use words.*
> —ROBERT LOWELL
> American poet, writing in 1964

secession, as Lincoln's running mate.

In July the war almost reached the steps of the White House. A Confederate force of 200,000 men led by General Jubal Early crossed the Potomac into Maryland, wrecking and burning mills, factories, and private homes on the way. Before Grant could send reinforcements, Early had cut all telegraph lines to Washington and pushed to within two miles of the city's outskirts. On July 12 Lincoln watched from the parapet at Fort Stevens as the two crack divisions sent by Grant pushed back the attackers. When an officer standing three feet from Lincoln was hit, the president was finally persuaded to seek cover. Early's troops were driven off, but, loaded with captured supplies, they escaped back into Virginia the next day.

As the summer of 1864 wore on, so did the war—stalemates, more deaths, more protests directed at the White House. Lincoln's chances for reelection looked slim.

The Democrats chose George McClellan to face Lincoln in November. McClellan would run on a peace platform aimed at restoring the Union with the institution of slavery intact. Most Republicans had many doubts about their party's prospects with Lincoln heading the ticket, and Lincoln himself thought he had little chance of defeating the popular general.

The news from Georgia on September 1, 1864, changed everything. "Atlanta," reported Sherman, "is ours." Lincoln credited the capture of this city, the symbol of the South's rebellion, to "Divine Favor," and designated the following Sunday a national day of thanksgiving.

Sherman's triumphant announcement followed an equally heartening bulletin from Mobile Bay, off the coast of Alabama. There, in the greatest naval action of the war, Union Admiral David G. Farragut attacked the Confederate fleet guarding Mobile, the South's strategically essential port. Mobile Bay, which was guarded by three major forts, was also thickly sown with mines, which were known at the time as torpedoes. Aiming for the South's most powerful ship, the 209-foot ironclad *Tennessee*, Far-

Mr. Lincoln is like a waiter in a large eating house where all the bells are ringing at once; he cannot serve them all at once and so some grumblers are to be expected.

—quoted from the *Cincinnati Gazette*, 1864

ragut responded to warnings about the mines with an order that became legendary: "Damn the torpedoes!" The forts surrendered on August 23, giving the Union navy full control of the Gulf of Mexico.

A few weeks later, Sheridan informed the government that he had given Early's forces a terrible beating in three separate engagements in Virginia's Shenandoah Valley. Republicans were jubilant. The Union victories had, it seemed, vindicated the president's policies. Some of Lincoln's most ardent opponents in the Republican party, men who had

The grim reality of war is captured in this photograph of wounded Union soldiers. Deeply moved by the sight of his bloodied and bandaged troops limping back to Washington following their defeat at Bull Run, Lincoln became even more determined to inflict a crushing and final defeat on the Confederacy.

JEFF DAVIS'S NOVEMBER NIGHTMARE.

An 1864 political cartoon portrays a frightened Jefferson Davis haunted by the prospect of Lincoln's reelection. Lincoln's November 8, 1864, victory over pro-slavery Democrat George B. McClellan crushed the Southerners' hopes that a president sympathetic to their interests might yet be elected and effect the repeal of Lincoln's emancipation legislation.

criticized him incessantly, now rallied to his side.

Lincoln himself engaged in skillful, though sometimes heavy-handed political activity: he ordered his field commanders to ensure that thousands of troops who were known to support him were sent home to vote, and he stiffened the resolve of the waverers in the Republican ranks by promising them important appointments. It all worked out handsomely. On November 8, 1864, Lincoln swamped McClellan in the electoral college, 212 to 21. He carried the soldiers' votes by overwhelming totals.

On January 31, 1865, Lincoln got his wish for a constitutional amendment outlawing slavery. Under considerable pressure from the White House, the U.S. House of Representatives narrowly passed the Thirteenth Amendment to the Constitution, a measure already approved by the Senate. With Lincoln's signature and subsequent ratification by the states, the amendment would forever abolish slavery in the United States.

Every Republican in the House voted "yea." When the clerk read the results, a roar went up on the floor. House members, many in tears, threw their arms around each other; women in the galleries waved their handkerchiefs. Across the country, blacks gathered to sing and offer prayers of thanks. William Lloyd Garrison, the sternly abolitionist Boston newspaper editor who had often criticized Lincoln for what he considered the president's lack of commitment on the issue of slavery, now gave the "humble railsplitter of Illinois" a new title: "Presidential Chainbreaker for millions of the oppressed." Lincoln called the passing of the amendment a "great moral victory."

On March 4, 1865, Abraham Lincoln once again took his place on the inaugural platform outside the Capitol. An eternity, it seemed, had passed since he last stood there, calling for reason and peace. He looked much older now, the worries of a lifetime etched on his drawn, deeply lined face.

On that day, Lincoln was a new man in the eyes of many Americans, one who had earned their trust and respect. In his search for meaning in the war,

Lincoln said, he had come to see the whole wrenching struggle as God's punishment for the sin of slavery. "This mighty scourge of war," he declared, was the price the nation had to pay, both North and South, for the centuries of injustice inflicted on the black race. But now was the hour for healing: "With malice toward none; with charity for all; with firmness in the right, as God gives us to see the right, let us strive on to finish the work we are in; to bind up the nation's wounds; to care for him who shall have borne the battle, and for his widow, and his orphan—to do all which may achieve and cherish a just, and a lasting peace, among ourselves, and with all nations."

From a platform in front of the Capitol, Abraham Lincoln delivers his second inaugural address on March 4, 1865. With former slave Frederick Douglass in the audience, Lincoln said that he prayed that the Civil War would "speedily pass away," but not until slavery was finally destroyed.

13

"To Bind Up the Nation's Wounds"

Spring 1865. The Northern armies, like a relentless blue tide, swept into the heart of the South, cutting a broad path of destruction. Its cities, towns, and fields aflame, its armies depleted, the Confederacy was doomed.

On Sunday, April 2, Grant broke through Lee's defenses at Petersburg, Virginia. Jefferson Davis, who was attending church in Richmond, received the news when a courier rushed in with a fearful message from Lee: "I advise that all preparation be made for leaving Richmond tonight."

As Davis and the Confederate government evacuated Richmond, the Southerners burned bridges and warehouses behind them. High winds swept the flames downtown. A Confederate gunner remembered the "miles on miles of fire; mountain piled on mountain of black smoke . . . one ceaseless babble of human voices, crying, shouting, cursing; one mighty pandemonium of woe." On the morning of April 3, a wave of blue uniforms poured into the blackened city. The Confederate flag above the state capitol was lowered and replaced by the Stars and Stripes.

On April 4 Lincoln toured the still-smoldering

Thomas Jefferson (1743–1826), third president of the United States, whose philosophy served as a source of inspiration for Lincoln. Lincoln, who read of Jefferson and the American Revolution during his days on the prairie, sought to preserve the Union and the American experiment in democracy for which the nation's Founding Fathers had fought with immense dedication.

The ruins of the Confederate capital, Richmond, Virginia, mark the conclusion of the Civil War. When Confederate troops evacuated the city, they burned bridges and warehouses behind them. A week later, General Lee surrendered, confirming a final victory for the North.

Robert E. Lee (center, seated at left) surrenders to Ulysses S. Grant (center, seated at right) at a house in Appomattox, Virginia, on April 9, 1865. Lincoln had instructed Grant to make the terms of surrender as merciful as possible.

city. As the president, dressed in black and sporting his customary stovepipe hat, picked his way through the burned-out rubble, a column of cheering blacks followed. A cavalry escort took him to the Confederate executive mansion. In the abandoned office of Jefferson Davis, Lincoln sat for a moment, lost in thought.

Less than a week later it was all over. Trapped near the Virginia village of Appomattox, with the massive federal army preparing a final assault, Lee informed Grant that he was ready to surrender.

On April 9, 1865, the white-haired Confederate general, wearing a full-dress uniform and jewel-studded sword, met his rumpled, mud-spattered Northern counterpart in the bare parlor of a house in Appomattox. Grant wrote the terms of surrender in accordance with Lincoln's instructions: "Give them the most liberal terms," the president had said. "Let them have their horses to plow with, and . . . their guns to shoot crows with. I want no one punished." Lee and Grant, each deeply respectful of the other's abilities, shook hands. "This," said Lee of the Union terms, "will do much toward conciliating our people."

When the Union artillery began to fire salutes after the meeting, Grant ordered them stopped. "The war," he said, "is over; the rebels are our countrymen again." Grant's official dispatch to Washington read: "General Lee surrendered the Army of Northern Virginia this afternoon on terms proposed by myself."

The Confederacy's president was less realistic

than his general in chief. Davis, who had slipped away from Richmond ahead of the Union army, headed further south, still hoping to regroup his forces. Even after Johnston surrendered to Sherman at the end of April, Davis refused to accept defeat. "Three thousand brave men," he said in a desperate plea to a group of cavalry officers in South Carolina, on May 3, "are enough for a nucleus around which the whole people will rally." Davis's officers knew better; they laid down their arms. After his capture by federal troops in Georgia on May 10, Davis was imprisoned for two years.

Following Lee's surrender, celebrations erupted all across the North. In Washington, Lincoln walked through downtown streets lit with torches, thronged with people. In his diary, Secretary of the Navy Gideon Welles wrote: "Guns are firing, bells ringing, flags flying, men laughing, children cheering, all, all are jubilant."

On the night of April 11, hundreds of people gathered on the White House lawn to hear the president speak from an upstairs window. Lincoln talked of the immense challenge that lay before the country. Competing interests would have to be reconciled; the desire for revenge would have to be eradicated. Seven years earlier he had said: "A house divided against itself cannot stand." Now, hundreds of thousands of deaths later, the awesome task of rebuilding lay ahead. (The nation lost 618,000 soldiers in the Civil War, approximately equal to the total in all other U.S. wars, including Vietnam, combined.) The job of reconstructing the conquered South "is fraught with great difficulty," Lincoln declared. "We simply must begin with, and mold from, disorganized and discordant elements."

The peace that would come out of the war, Lincoln believed, had to be humane, constructive, and generous enough to ensure unity. It should not provoke further violence and hatred. To Generals Grant and Sherman, just before the end of the war, Lincoln had talked about the end of hostilities and the policies he would follow in his dealings with the rebels. Let them return to their farms and shops, let them pledge their loyalty to the United States, let them

The man's appearance, his pedigree, his coarse low jokes and anecdotes, his vulgar similes and his frivolity, are a disgrace to the seat he holds.
—JOHN WILKES BOOTH
Lincoln's assassin

reestablish state governments, he had said. "Let 'em up easy."

For Lincoln himself, the end of the war seemed a time for a new beginning. He talked to Mary about the years ahead, when, with the second term behind them, they would have time to travel. He looked forward to the day when he would be able to practice in Chicago or Springfield, when he could finally relax with his old friends, swapping jokes and stories.

Lincoln had taken many terrible blows between 1861 and 1865, but he was still standing. Author Harriet Beecher Stowe had written: "Surrounded by all sorts of conflicting claims, by traitors, by half-hearted, timid men, by Border States men, and Free States men, by radical Abolitionists and Conservatives, he has listened to all, weighed the words of all, waited, observed, yielded now here and now there, but in the main kept one inflexible, honest

purpose, and drawn the national ship through."

Lincoln had sought to preserve something he had cherished all his life, something he had deeply respected since those early days on the prairie when he first read of Jefferson and the American Revolution. He had sought to preserve the Union and to ensure the continuation of the American experiment in democracy. "I happen temporarily to occupy this big White House," Lincoln declared. "I am a living witness that any one of your children may look to come here as my father's child has . . . that each of you may have through this free government which we have enjoyed, an open field and a fair chance for your industry, enterprise and intelligence; that you may all have equal privileges in the race of life. . . ."

Good Friday, April 14, 1865, was a lovely spring day. The dogwoods were in bloom. The Lincolns

Abraham Lincoln is shot by Southern sympathizer John Wilkes Booth while attending a play at Ford's Theater, in Washington, on April 14, 1865. Lincoln died at 7:22 A.M. on the following day.

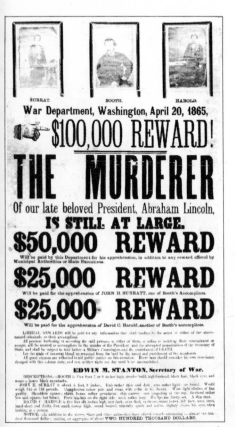

A poster offers rewards for the capture of Booth and his accomplices. Booth was killed several days after the assassination in a gun battle with federal troops in Virginia.

planned a carriage ride together. That evening they would attend Ford's Theater on Tenth Street to see an English comedy called "Our American Cousin."

In the morning the president, seeming more relaxed than usual, met with the cabinet and General Grant. They discussed plans for the reconstruction of the South. Although he realized that a strong military occupation would be necessary during the rebuilding process in the South, Lincoln told them he preferred there be "no bloody work," such as war trials or firing squads. (The only person executed as a war criminal in the aftermath of the conflict was the commandant of the prisoner-of-war camp in Andersonville, Georgia. Captain Henry Wirz, a Swiss immigrant, received the death sentence for the countless cruelties that he had inflicted upon captured Union soldiers.)

At 9:00 P.M., Lincoln and Mary arrived at Ford's Theater, receiving an ovation from the audience as they entered the flag-draped presidential box. An hour later, a shot rang out. A slender, black-haired, moustached actor named John Wilkes Booth had entered the presidential box, leveled a six-inch brass revolver at the back of the president's head, and fired. Booth then leapt from the box onto the stage, where he waved his pistol and shouted, *Sic semper tyrannis!*—(Latin for "Thus always to tyrants"). His leg was broken, but he was able to rush out to a horse waiting in the alley.

As the unconscious Lincoln was carried to a house across the street, an accomplice of Booth tried unsuccessfully to kill Secretary of State Seward at his home. Booth, a wildly emotional Southern sympathizer, had recruited several others in an elaborate scheme to kill Lincoln, Seward, and Vice-President Johnson. Only Booth, assigned to assassinate Lincoln, was successful. He, along with the others, would soon pay for their crimes with their lives.

Abraham Lincoln died the following day—April 15, 1865—at 7:22 A.M. He had never recovered consciousness. After a funeral service in the White House on April 19, his body lay in state in the Capitol for two days. A long funeral train was soon on its way to Illinois, virtually retracing the route Lincoln had taken to Washington four years earlier. Thousands lined the tracks to watch in silence as the train slowly passed. Never before had an American president fallen victim to assassination. Stunned by the tragedy, Americans grieved at their loss.

Lincoln's coffin traveled 1,700 miles in its roundabout journey to Illinois. More than 7 million people viewed it at the many stops the train made along the way. As the train later rolled into Ohio, newspapers announced that Booth had died in a blazing barn in Virginia, following a gun battle with federal troops.

At last, in Springfield, where Lincoln had lived so much of his life, mourning friends, associates, and strangers, white and black, solemnly paid their last respects at the open coffin of the slain president.

The poet Walt Whitman, remembering the flaming torches, the sea of faces, the tolling bells, wrote: "I mourn'd, and yet shall mourn with ever-returning spring. . . ."

The train bearing Lincoln's body prepares to leave Washington for Illinois on April 21, 1865. Thousands lined the tracks to pay silent homage to the deceased president as the train made its 1,700-mile journey. Lincoln was buried in Springfield.

Further Reading

Current, Richard. *The Lincoln Nobody Knows.* New York: McGraw-Hill Book Co., 1958.

Donald, David. *Lincoln Reconsidered.* New York: Random House, Inc., 1947.

Fehrenbacher, Don. *Abraham Lincoln: A Documentary Portrait through His Speeches and Writings.* New York: New American Library, 1964.

Larant, Stefan. *Lincoln: A Picture Story of His Life.* New York: W.W. Norton & Co., Inc., 1952.

Nevins, Allan, ed. *Lincoln and the Gettysburg Address.* Urbana, Illinois: University of Illinois Press, 1964.

Oates, Stephen B. *With Malice Toward None.* New York: Harper & Row Publishers, Inc., 1977.

Pole, J. R. *Abraham Lincoln.* London: Oxford University Press, 1964.

Sandburg, Carl. *Abraham Lincoln: The Prairie Years and the War Years.* New York: Dell Publishing Co., Inc., 1959.

Thomas, Benjamin. *Abraham Lincoln.* New York: Alfred A. Knopf, Inc., 1952.

280 words

Chronology

Feb. 12, 1809	Born Abraham Lincoln in Hardin County, Kentucky
1832	Serves as captain in Illinois militia
1834	Elected, as Whig party candidate, to first of four terms in Illinois state legislature
March 1, 1837	Admitted to the bar in Springfield, Illinois, where he subsequently opens a law practice
Nov. 4, 1842	Marries Mary Todd in Springfield
1846	Elected to the U.S. House of Representatives
1854	Congress passes Kansas-Nebraska Act, which allows new territories to determine independently whether to permit slavery
Feb. 28, 1854	Republican party formed, with the primary objective of opposing slavery in new territories
1858	Lincoln, running as the Republican party candidate, loses bid for U.S. Senate to Stephen A. Douglas
Nov. 6, 1860	Elected 16th president of the United States
Feb. 8, 1861	Representatives of seven Southern states adopt a constitution and unite as the Confederate States of America
April 12, 1861	Confederates fire first shots of the Civil War, shelling Fort Sumter, South Carolina
July 21, 1861	Confederates defeat Union army at Bull Run in the Civil War's first battle
Sept. 17, 1862	Union army defeats Confederates at Antietam Creek, Maryland
Jan. 1, 1863	Lincoln signs the Emancipation Proclamation, abolishing slavery
July 1863	Battle of Gettysburg
Nov. 19, 1863	Lincoln delivers the Gettysburg Address
March 4, 1865	Begins second term as president—after winning election against Union General George McClellan—with inaugural address calling for "malice toward none"
April 9, 1865	Confederate General Robert E. Lee surrenders to Union General Ulysses S. Grant at Appomattox
April 14, 1865	Lincoln is shot by John Wilkes Booth at Ford's Theater, Washington, D.C.
April 15, 1865	Lincoln dies, aged 56

Index

Roger Bruns is Director of Publications of the National Historical Publications and Records Commission in Washington, D.C. His books include *Knights of the Road: A Hobo History,* published by Methuen, Inc. He is also the author of *Thomas Jefferson* in the Chelsea House series WORLD LEADERS   PAST & PRESENT.

Arthur M. Schlesinger, jr., taught history at Harvard for many years and is currently Albert Schweitzer Professor of the Humanities at City University of New York. He is the author of numerous highly praised works in American history and has twice been awarded the Pulitzer Prize. He served in the White House as special assistant to presidents Kennedy and Johnson.